GETTING TO GRIPS WITH

KU-215-925

Vocabulary

CATHERINE HILTON
MARGARET HYDER

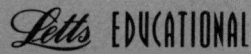
Letts EDUCATIONAL

First published 1992

Editorial team
Rachel Grant, Andrew Thraves, Angela Royal

Design team
Frank Greenyer, Jonathan Barnard

Text © Catherine Hilton and Margaret Hyder

© BPP (Letts Educational) Ltd
Aldine House, Aldine Place, 142-144 Uxbridge Road, London W12 8AW

British Library Cataloguing in Publication Data

Hilton, Catherine
  Vocabulary. – (Getting to Grips)
  I. Title II. Hyder, Margaret III. Series
  428. 10222

ISBN 1 85758 093 1

Printed and bound in Great Britain by BPCC Wheatons Ltd

Authors' note: The suggestions made in Chapter 6 about tackling the comprehension paper are our own and not those of an AEB examiner.

Acknowledgements

Pages 21, 36, entries from *The Collins Paperback English Dictionary*, William Collins Sons & Co Ltd, 1990, with acknowledgements to Collins English Dictionaries; pages 17, 24, 28, 29, 32, 33, 35, entries from *Chambers Concise Dictionaries*, W&R Chambers, Edinburgh 1991; pages 23, 24, 30 entries from *The Concise Oxford Dictionary* (8th ed., 1990) by permission of Oxford University Press; page 40, extract from *The Dictionary of Synonyms and Antonyms*, Pan Books; page 38, extract from Iris Murdoch, *The Philosopher's Son*, Chatto and Windus; pages 36, 41, 42, 47 entries from *Collins Paperback Thesaurus in A–Z form*; pages 47, 75, 78, entries from *Penguin English Dictionary*; page 54 extract from Graham Green, *A Burnt-Out Case*, William Heinemann Ltd, © 1960 Verdant S.A.; page 57 extract from *Eureka!* Thames & Hudson Ltd; page 58, 'C&T Develops Multiprocessing Design' by Tom Yager, *Byte* magazine, April 1991; page 66–7, from City and Guilds specimen multiple choice paper – Communication Skills 361; page 67–8, from AEB GCE 'O' level paper, June 1986, English Language syllabus 1, paper 2; page 138, extract from Barbara Pym, *Excellent Women*, reproduced with the permission of the Estate of Barbara Pym and Jonathan Cape; page 144, extract from Tom Vernon, *Fat Man on a Bicycle*, reproduced by permission of Michael Joseph Ltd; page 144, extract from Mark Wallington, *500 Mile Walkies*, Hutchinson Books Ltd; page 145, extract from an article by Birna Helgadottir, *The European*, 23/25 August 1991.

Contents

How to Use this Book

The aim of this book is to enhance your vocabulary, foster a love and appreciation of words and give you the confidence to use a wide and vivid vocabulary.

It is advisable to work systematically through the chapters in Section 1 as they establish the skills and knowledge required in the next two sections.

Section 1 gives you advice about improving your vocabulary by:

▶ the sensible use of dictionaries and thesauruses

▶ wide and active reading

▶ attentive listening

▶ being aware of words which are commonly misused or confused

Section 2 looks at a selection of words which, through overuse, have become hackneyed and imprecise. It suggests ways of avoiding them and enriching our conversation and writing with less common synonyms. You can work straight through Section 2 or you can dip into it – selecting those words that you feel are most useful and relevant to you. To get the most out of this section, you will need to have a dictionary and thesaurus at your side for quick reference.

By the time you have studied the previous two sections, you will be sufficiently confident to embark upon the formal and creative writing tasks in Section 3, where you are introduced to a variety of words to fit specific situations. Advice is given about vocabulary for

creative and informative writing

formal letters

reports

essays

After you have worked through the book, you may find it difficult to recall the meanings and uses of all the words you have encountered and will need to go back to certain chapters to refresh your memory. Or you may be 'lost for words' and find this book provides you with a useful reference source.

1
Introducing Vocabulary

English is a living language and so it is difficult to be precise about the exact number of words in the language; new words are constantly being added while others disappear through lack of use. It is estimated that there are approximately half a million words in the language, yet most of us use less than twenty thousand of these words.

We each have our own personal vocabulary which is unique to us. Obviously there is a great deal of overlap from one person to another, but the exact set of words that one person has in his vocabulary will be distinct from the next person's. We have absorbed this personal set from our own special environment.

As children our vocabulary grows rapidly without, it seems, any real effort, but as adults our vocabulary increases more slowly and can remain fairly static unless we have a reason or make a concerted effort to enlarge it. We only have to flick through a dictionary, listen to a programme about an unfamiliar subject or read a challenging book to realise the limitations of our own vocabulary.

Although you will unconsciously absorb new words throughout your life, if you want your vocabulary to increase significantly then you will have to take positive steps. Improving your vocabulary is an active and rewarding process.

Words are powerful tools. We need a rich supply so that we can select the correct tools for the job as we would with any other task we tackled. We need a good vocabulary.

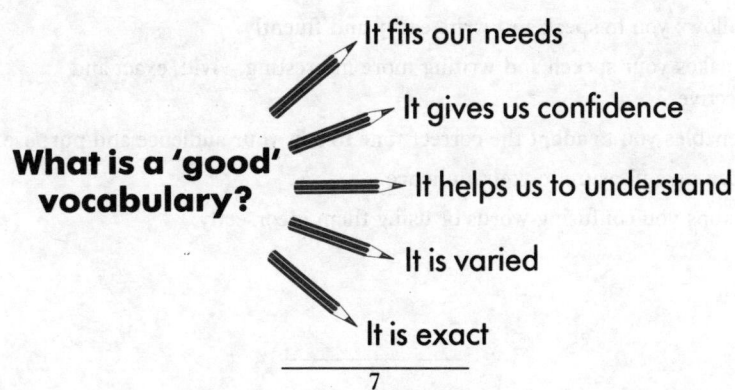

What is a 'good' vocabulary?

It fits our needs

It gives us confidence

It helps us to understand

It is varied

It is exact

It fits our needs

Each of us needs a vocabulary which allows us to cope with our lifestyle confidently and with ease. When we change jobs, acquire new interests or alter our lifestyle we often need to learn new words.

It gives us confidence

Knowing that we have the vocabulary to cope with a variety of situations helps us to be more confident. Most of us feel ill at ease when we are 'out of our depth'.

It helps us to understand

The larger our vocabulary, the easier it is for us to understand a wide range of speech and writing.

It is varied

If we keep using the same words in speech or writing, it can be boring both for us and for our audience; we need a variety of words to choose from. Words of similar meanings are called **synonyms**. It is useful to have a range of synonyms at our command as they can make the speaking and writing process easier and our speech and writing more interesting and fluent.

It is exact

A good writer or speaker uses the minimum of words to impart his message. Every word counts and must be carefully selected. If we want our message to be clear, exact and unambiguous, we must pay special attention to the words we choose.

Why is a good vocabulary important?

▶ It helps you understand the exact meaning of what you hear and read so that there is no misunderstanding on your part.

▶ It allows you to speak and write easily and fluently.

▶ It makes your speech and writing more interesting, vivid, exact and effective.

▶ It enables you to adopt the correct tone to suit your audience and purpose.

▶ It can give pleasure to your audience.

▶ It stops you confusing words or using them incorrectly.

- It can give you a range of precise words to use in formal writing tasks such as letters, reports, summaries and essays.
- It allows you to impart shades of meaning and colour which are particularly useful in creative or narrative writing.

How can you acquire a good vocabulary?

Plan your campaign

Practise

Be determined

Understand prefixes

Be alive to words

Listen actively

Acquiring a good vocabulary

Be curious

Do word games

Read responsively

Use a thesaurus

Use a dictionary

Make your own personal dictionary

Plan your campaign

Your vocabulary will continue to increase throughout life if you provide the right conditions for its growth. It isn't something that will necessarily happen without a determined effort on your part. First of all, you need to understand your own reasons for wanting to improve.

** Make a list of all the reasons why you want to improve your vocabulary.

Make a second list of all the advantages of an improved vocabulary for *you*.

As you work through this book, you may want to add to your lists or tick off some of the advantages as you begin to achieve them.

To be successful you need to be alive to words and curious about them. Try to find ways of encountering new words by listening, reading and taking part in word games. Develop a strategy for researching all the new words you find.

We use the term 'new word' to refer to a word which isn't in your natural vocabulary. Your natural vocabulary consists of the words you use confidently because you understand their meaning and usage. There will be many words that you have heard and seen but you may not be completely certain about their meaning so you don't use them; they are not part of your natural vocabulary.

When you find a new word, you need to research it by

> finding out what it means and
>
> considering how to use it in sentences
>
> before incorporating it into your natural vocabulary.

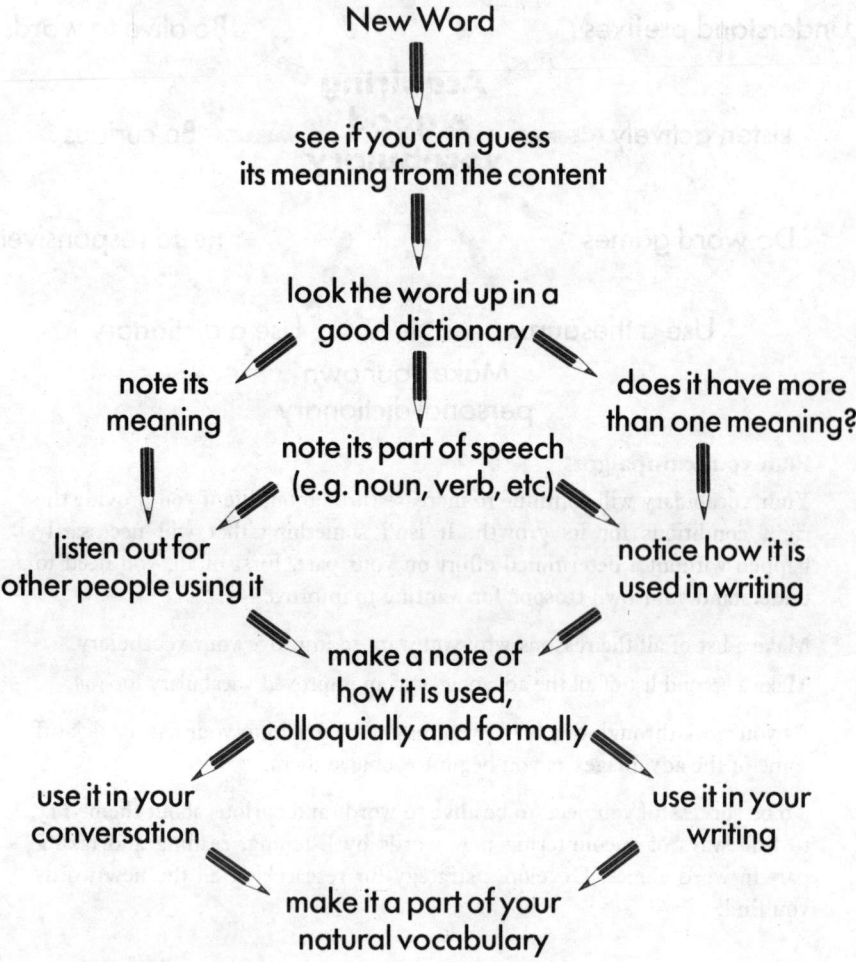

New Word

see if you can guess its meaning from the content

look the word up in a good dictionary

note its meaning

note its part of speech (e.g. noun, verb, etc)

does it have more than one meaning?

listen out for other people using it

notice how it is used in writing

make a note of how it is used, colloquially and formally

use it in your conversation

use it in your writing

make it a part of your natural vocabulary

Make your own personal dictionary

You will need to be organised and devise your own way of storing new words. An alphabetically indexed book or an alphabetically arranged card filing system can be used. Your entry may look something like this.

furore (noun)
wild enthusiasm
wild excitement
an uproar

synonyms—frenzy
commotion
disturbance
outburst

Listen actively

We learn to talk by listening to others and imitating them. Words are linked to objects, situations and emotions. Children constantly ask, "What does that mean?" It is readily accepted that children need to ask questions in order to learn and an enquiring child is usually said to be an intelligent one.

As adults we often fail to ask, "What does it mean?" This does not necessarily mean that we have less enquiring minds but we are often embarrassed to ask others what is meant by certain things they say or words they use. They might think that we are ignorant or uneducated. We can sometimes only ask close friends or family members – people we trust. This failure to question can prevent us from increasing our vocabulary and understanding.

Be an active listener. Listen carefully to all the words you hear and if you don't feel you can ask about unfamiliar words then try to remember them or note them down so that you can research them later.

You can spend your time wisely in railway carriages, restaurants, at bus stops and other public places by listening to what others are saying and isolating unfamiliar words. Often you can guess the meaning of such words from the rest of the conversation or by the speaker's expression or tone of voice, but it is always a good idea to check the precise meaning of these words in a dictionary later. One new word can lead to another.

Radio and television provide a rich source of new words, especially if you listen to a wide range of news programmes, documentaries, discussions and subjects which are outside of your usual range of interests. It helps if you have a piece of paper and a pen to hand so that you can note down new words to check later. This shouldn't be irksome or spoil your pleasure in the programmes; in fact it could even enhance your enjoyment.

To be an effective listener, concentrate, note down, follow up and use the word.

Read responsively

Read as much as possible; reading helps you to enlarge your vocabulary. Try to read a wide variety of good magazines, newspapers and books so that you will be presented with an interesting range of vocabulary.

Whenever you are reading, whether for pleasure, as part of your work, or for information, be aware of new words. It is all too easy only to grasp the gist of what we are reading and so ignore new words. Be prepared to collect new words and research them.

It can spoil the enjoyment of your reading if you stop to look up every unfamiliar word. If the book is yours, underline new words in pencil so that you can follow them up later. However, it is inadvisable to do this in borrowed books – it may make you unpopular with the librarian!

** Read each of the sentences opposite and check that you *really* understand the meaning of each underlined word. (Could you clearly explain its meaning to someone who was unfamiliar with this word?)

Follow these steps.

Try to guess the meaning of the word from its context.

Look it up in your dictionary.

Complete an entry for it in your
personal dictionary.

Choose the meaning which best
suits your context.

1 The refugees were offered <u>succour</u> and support in neighbouring countries.

2 There was such a <u>plethora</u> of parties at the election that the peasants found it difficult to know which party to vote for.

3 Parents are <u>revered</u> in Chinese families.

4 Peter was described by his teachers as a 'wild, <u>exuberant</u>, hot-headed boy'.

5 Holidays abroad are no longer a <u>prerogative</u> of the idle rich.

6 The plans are to <u>regenerate</u> derelict urban areas.

Use a dictionary and thesaurus

If you are serious about improving your vocabulary, you need a good dictionary and thesaurus. Chapters 2, 3 and 4 will give you advice about which dictionary and thesaurus to choose and how to use them effectively. A dictionary will help you to understand the meaning of a new word and a thesaurus will allow you to follow up your research by showing you a range of synonyms for a given word.

If you look back at the card-index entry on page 11, you will see that the entry includes a short list of synonyms. By using your dictionary and thesaurus you will be able to make a detailed entry in your filing system for any new word.

Understanding prefixes

A prefix is a group of letters that is added to the beginning of a word. Each prefix has a meaning. **Knowing the meaning of a prefix can help you to work out the meaning of an unfamiliar word.** A good dictionary will give you the meaning of a prefix.

e.g. The prefix **mal** means bad or badly, so

maladjusted means poorly or badly adjusted,

malfunction means to work imperfectly, and

malodour means a bad smell.

By understanding what the prefix means and by looking at the sentence in which a word is used, it is often possible to guess the meaning of a word.

Word games

Any games involving words can be helpful because they make you aware of the variety of words and help you to develop mastery over them. Quick crosswords which involve word substitution are particularly useful. Make a habit of tackling the quick crossword in a quality newspaper each day. If you aren't very successful at first, keep trying as you will improve with practice. It is a good idea to buy a crossword dictionary as this will help you to complete the puzzle and expose you to new words.

Practice

As with any skill, practice is essential.

Try to use your new words as much as possible, both in speech and writing. If you are not certain that you are using a word correctly, try it out on your friends and family first. Listen and look out for the word being used by other people in their speech and writing.

Aim to make your conversation more exact and interesting by avoiding vague and overused words, e.g. nice, lovely, thing, get. Substitute more exact and interesting words. Deliver your message as briefly and vividly as possible.

Make it your task to learn five new words each day. If you exhaust the list of words gained from your reading and listening, browse through your dictionary and select words. Choose words which will be useful to you and ignore the obscure words.

Go back over your personal dictionary from time to time to test yourself. Write an interesting sentence for any of the words that you are still concerned about.

When you complete a piece of writing, check it through thoroughly and underline any loose words or phrases. See if you can replace any of these by more exact words. This doesn't mean that you have to replace them with long or complicated words – a simple word can be just as exact. You are not using vocabulary to impress people but to produce clear, concise and effective writing.

** Start to build up your list of words to research by selecting 26 words from your dictionary – one for each letter of the alphabet. Use the guide words at the top of each page and make your choice from these words.

** Think of a topic and make a list of all the words you know connected with it.

e.g. law – decree nisi, abet, plaintiff, statute, waive, negligence, executor, felony, mitigation, disclaimer. . . .

You will probably include words that you have heard frequently but perhaps you are a little vague about their meanings. Be honest with yourself and check all those you are uncertain about.

Over to you

A wide vocabulary can make you feel more confident and give you and your audience pleasure so it is worth spending time developing it. You need a voracious appetite for words, so:

read widely

listen carefully

do crosswords and other word games

cultivate an enquiring mind

use your dictionary and thesaurus sensibly

learn five new words each day

use your new words whenever possible

start building up your personal dictionary now!

2
Understanding Dictionaries

If you are determined to improve your vocabulary, then you must have at least one good dictionary and feel confident about using it. A dictionary is the effective writer's and speaker's paint-box of words: an essential tool.

How can a good dictionary help?

meaning	It will help you to understand the meaning or meanings of words.
pronunciation	It will show you how words are normally pronounced.
parts of speech	It will indicate the part of speech of each entry; this helps you to use words in their correct context.
spelling	It will enable you to check the spelling of words and any changes of spelling that occur when suffixes are added. e.g. dial, dialling, dialled.
origin	A brief history of each word is included so that you are able to appreciate the origin of each entry.
related words and phrases	When you look up a word, you will often find related words under the entry. These can help to boost your vocabulary and increase your mastery of words if you are sufficiently curious to follow them up.

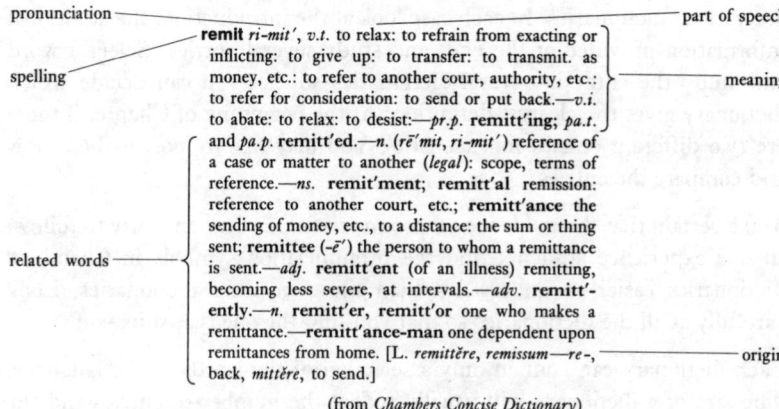

pronunciation ——————

spelling

meaning

part of speech

related words

remit *ri-mit'*, *v.t.* to relax: to refrain from exacting or inflicting: to give up: to transfer: to transmit. as money, etc.: to refer to another court, authority, etc.: to refer for consideration: to send or put back.—*v.i.* to abate: to relax: to desist:—*pr.p.* **remitt'ing**; *pa.t.* and *pa.p.* **remitt'ed.**—*n.* (*rē'mit, ri-mit'*) reference of a case or matter to another (*legal*): scope, terms of reference.—*ns.* **remit'ment**; **remitt'al** remission: reference to another court, etc.; **remitt'ance** the sending of money, etc., to a distance: the sum or thing sent; **remittee** (*-ē'*) the person to whom a remittance is sent.—*adj.* **remitt'ent** (of an illness) remitting, becoming less severe, at intervals.—*adv.* **remitt'ently.**—*n.* **remitt'er, remitt'or** one who makes a remittance.—**remitt'ance-man** one dependent upon remittances from home. [L. *remittĕre, remissum*—*re-*, back, *mittĕre*, to send.]

origin

(from *Chambers Concise Dictionary*)

A dictionary is a fascinating storehouse of words which, if used effectively, will not only develop your vocabulary but will also enhance your love of words.

Choosing a dictionary

There is an excellent range of dictionaries in most book shops and it is advisable to spend some time selecting one. Beware of cheap 'special purchase' dictionaries which often have a very limited range of words, incomplete and even misleading definitions, and give no information about inflexions (changes to spelling).

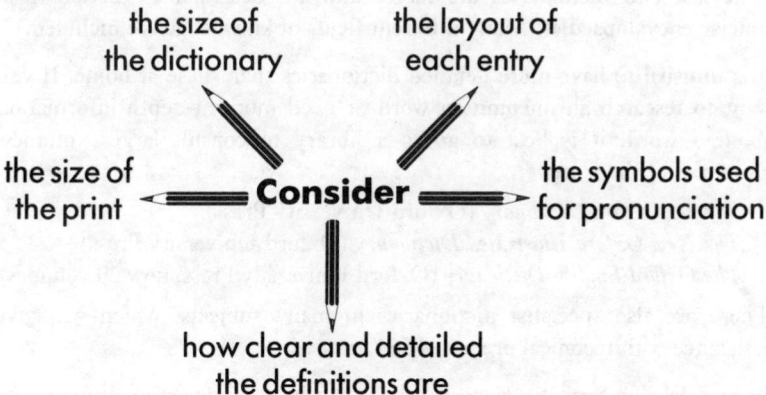

the size of
the dictionary

the layout of
each entry

the size of
the print

Consider

the symbols used
for pronunciation

how clear and detailed
the definitions are

Choice of a dictionary is a personal matter; you want one that fits your needs and is easy for you to use. It may help if you look at other people's dictionaries and ask their advice, or go to your local library so that you can use various dictionaries. In each case look at the introduction, the additional information provided at the end, and study several entries. Select a word and study the entry in several dictionaries so that you can decide which dictionary gives the clearest definition. At the beginning of Chapter 3 there are two different entries for 'acoustic'. You may like to look at these now and compare the entries.

Make certain that the guidance on pronunciation is clear and easy to follow. In our experience students find the pronunciation symbols in Chambers dictionaries easier to understand than those in other dictionaries. Look carefully at all the dictionaries so that you find the one that suits you.

Each dictionary can contain only a selection of the words in the language. The size of a dictionary will usually reflect the number of entries and the amount of detail about each entry. Pocket dictionaries are very useful to carry with you, but you will need a larger, more detailed dictionary for your vocabulary research. Good examples are:

> *The Concise Oxford Dictionary* (Oxford University Press)
> *The New Penguin Dictionary* (Penguin)
> *Chambers Concise Dictionary* (Chambers)
> *Collins Concise Dictionary* (Collins)
> *Collins Concise Dictionary Plus* (Collins)
> *The Cassell Concise English Dictionary* (Cassell)
> *The Collins English Dictionary* (Collins)
> *Oxford Reference Dictionary* (Oxford University Press)

(The last two dictionaries are larger and are designed as dictionaries/ concise encyclopaedias. Many different fields of knowledge are included.)

It is unusual to have more detailed dictionaries than these at home. If you want to research an uncommon word or need more in-depth information about a word, it is best to go to a library to consult larger volumes. Examples of these are:

> *Shorter Oxford Dictionary* (Oxford University Press)
> *The New Oxford Illustrated Dictionary* (Oxford University Press)
> *The Oxford English Dictionary* (Oxford University Press, now 20 volumes)

There are also specialist dictionaries in many subjects, which will give assistance with technical or specialised terms.

As you develop a greater curiosity about words, you may enjoy dipping into the increasing range of unusual dictionaries, for example:

> *The Penguin Dictionary of Curious and Interesting Words* (Penguin)
> *The Dictionary of Contemporary Slang* (Pan)

Le Mot Juste, The Penguin Dictionary of Foreign Terms & Phrases (Penguin)
A Dictionary of Eponyms (Oxford University Press). Eponyms are words derived from people's names. The meaning of each entry is explained and there is a short account of the originator.
Dictionary of Confusing Words & Meanings (Routledge & Kegan Paul)
A Dictionary of Euphemisms (Hamish Hamilton). A euphemism is the substitution of a mild or vague expression to describe an unpleasant, offensive or sensitive subject.
Newspeak, A Dictionary of Jargon (Routledge & Kegan Paul)

When you have chosen your dictionary, spend some time familiarising yourself with it. Start at the beginning and read the information in the introductory pages. You probably won't read every word but you need to become accustomed to the layout of your dictionary so that you can easily refer to the appropriate pages when you are trying to understand an entry.

Are there any difficulties?

Using a dictionary can be a time-consuming process unless you know your way around your own dictionary and can use it effectively.

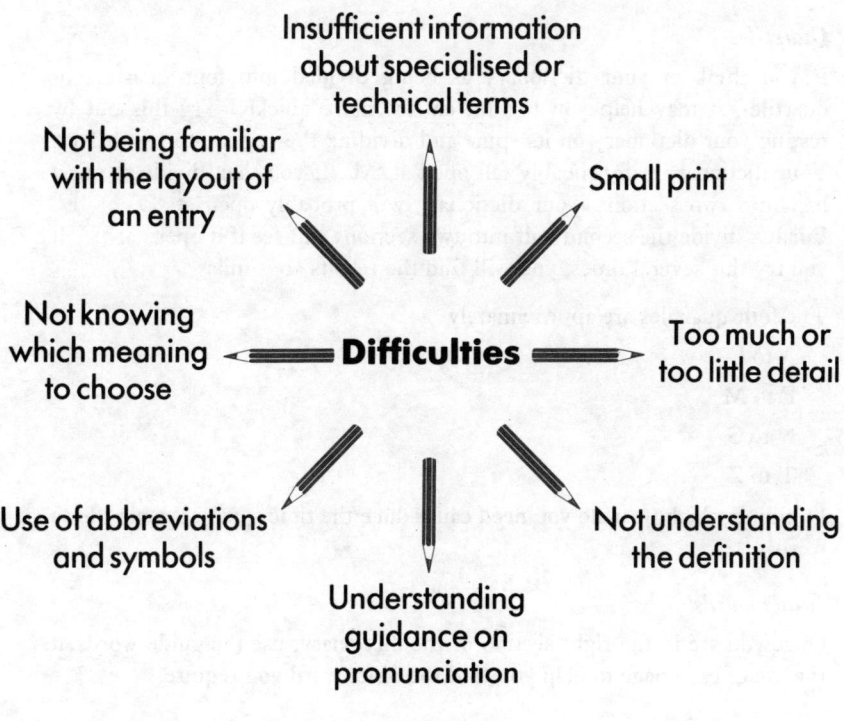

Making the most of your dictionary

If you are going to research words accurately and quickly, you need to be able to:

▶ find entries quickly

▶ understand the abbreviations and symbols

▶ understand the terms

▶ understand the entries (see Chapter 3)

Finding entries quickly

Unless you can find entries reasonably quickly, you may be discouraged from using your dictionary.

Alphabetical order

As all entries in a dictionary are arranged in alphabetical order, you need to be able to sequence the letters of the alphabet very quickly. Although you may be familiar with the order of the letters, you may find there are certain groups of letters which present difficulties when you are in a hurry. Sort out any such groups and improve your familiarity with the sequence.

Quartiles

If you think of your dictionary as being divided into four quarters or quartiles, it may help you to find entries more quickly. Try this out by resting your dictionary on its spine and dividing the pages into two halves. Your dictionary will probably fall open at 'M'. If you then divide the first half into two sections, your dictionary will probably open at 'D' or 'E'. Finally, divide the second half into two sections and see if it opens at 'S'. If you try this several times, you will find the results are similar.

The four quartiles are approximately

> A to E
> F to M
> N to S
> T to Z

Deciding which quartile you need can reduce the time spent searching for a word.

Guide words

Once you are in the right section of the dictionary, use the guide words at the top of each page to help you find the exact word you require.

copies of a book left unsold when demand ceases, which are sold at a reduced price, ∼ *vb.* 4. to sell (copies of a book as a remainder).

remains (rɪˈmeɪnz) *pl. n.* 1. any pieces that are left unused or still extant, as after use, consumption, or the passage of time: *archaeoligical remains.* 2. a corpse.

remake (ˈriːˌmeɪk) *n.* something that is made again, esp. a new version of an old film.

remand (rɪˈmɑːnd) *vb.* 1. *Law.* to send (a prisoner or accused person) back into custody to await trial. ∼ *n.* 2. the sending of a prisoner or accused person back into custody to await trial. 3. **on remand.** in custody or on bail awaiting trial.

remand centre *n.* (in Britain) an institution where accused people are detained while awaiting trial.

remark (rɪˈmɑːk) *vb.* 1. to pass a casual comment (about). 2. to perceive; observe; notice. ∼ *n.* 3. a brief casually expressed thought or opinion. 4. notice, comment, or observation: *the event passed without remark.*

remarkable (rɪˈmɑːkəbˀl) *adj.* 1. worthy of note or attention: *a remarkable achievement.* 2. striking or extraordinary: *a remarkable sight.* —reˈmarkably *adv.*

REME (ˈriːmɪ) Royal Electrical and Mechanical Engineers.

remedial (rɪˈmiːdɪəl) *adj.* 1. providing or intended as a remedy; curative. 2. of special teaching for slow learners: *remedial education.* —reˈmedially *adv.*

remedy (ˈrɛmɪdɪ) *n., pl.* **-dies.** (usually foll. by *for* or *against*). 1. any drug or agent that cures a disease or contols its symptoms. 2. anything that serves to cure defects, improve conditions, etc.: *a remedy for industrial disputes.* ∼ *vb.* 3. to relieve or cure (a disease). 4. to correct (a fault, error, etc.). —**remediable** (rɪˈmiːdɪəbˀl) *adj.*

remember (rɪˈmɛmbə) *vb.* 1. to become aware of (something forgotten) again. 2. to keep (an idea, intention, etc.) in one's mind: *remember to do one's shopping.* 3. to give money to (someone), as in a will or in tipping. 4. (foll. by *to*) to mention (a person's name) to another person, as by way of greeting: *remember me to your mother.* 5. to commemorate: *to remember the dead of the wars.*

remembrance (rɪˈmɛmbrəns) *n.* 1. a remembering or being remembered. 2. a memento or keepsake. 3. the act of honouring some past event or person.

Remembrance Day *n.* 1. (in Britain) Remembrance Sunday. 2. (in Canada) a statutory holiday observed on November 11 in memory of the dead of both World Wars.

Remembrance Sunday *n.* (in Britain) the Sunday closest to November 11th, on which the dead of both World Wars are commemorated.

remind (rɪˈmaɪnd) *vb.* (usually foll. by *of*) to cause (a person) to remember (something or to do something); put (a person) in mind (of someone or something): *remind me to phone home; flowers remind me of holidays.* —reˈminder *n.*

reminisce (ˌrɛmɪˈnɪs) *vb.* to talk or write about old times or past experience.

reminiscence (ˌrɛmɪˈnɪsəns) *n.* 1. the act of recalling or narrating past experiences. 2. (*often pl.*) some past experience, event or feeling that is recalled.

reminiscent (ˌrɛmɪˈnɪsənt) *adj.* 1. (foll. by *of*) stimulating memories (of) or comparisons (with). 2. characterized by reminiscence.

remiss (rɪˈmɪs) *adj.* lacking in attention to duty; negligent.

remission (rɪˈmɪʃən) *n.* 1. a reduction of the term of imprisonment, as for good conduct. 2. forgiveness for sin. 3. release from penalty or obligation. 4. lessening of intensity, as in the symptoms of a disease.

remit *vb.* (rɪˈmɪt), **-mitting, -mitted.** 1. to send (payment), as for goods or service, esp. by post. 2. *Law.* to send back (a case) to a lower court for further consideration. 3. to refrain from exacting or cancel (a penalty or punishment). 4. to slacken or ease off; abate. 5. *Archaic.* to forgive (crime or sins). ∼ *n.* (ˈriːmɪt). 6. area of authority (of a committee, inquiry, etc.).

remittance (rɪˈmɪtəns) *n.* money sent, esp. by post, as payment.

remittent (rɪˈmɪtᵊnt) *adj.* (of a disease) periodically less severe.

remix *vb.* (riːˈmɪks). 1. to change the relative volume and prominence of the individual performer's parts of (a recording). ∼ *n.* (ˈriːmɪks). 2. a remixed version of a recording.

remnant (ˈrɛmnənt) *n.* 1. (*often pl.*) a part left over. 2. a surviving trace or vestige: *a remnant of imperialism.* 3. a piece of material from the end of a roll.

remonstrance (rɪˈmɒnstrəns) *n.* 1. the act of remonstrating. 2. a protest or reproof, esp. a petition protesting against something.

remonstrate (ˈrɛmənˌstreɪt) *vb.* to argue in protest or objection: *to remonstrate with the government.* —ˌremonˈstration *n.*

remorse (rɪˈmɔːs) *n.* 1. a sense of deep regret and guilt for some misdeed. 2. pity; compassion. —reˈmorseful *adj.*

remote (rɪˈmaʊt) *adj.* 1. far away; distant

(from *The Collins Paperback English Dictionary*)

This shows you that 'remains' is the first complete entry and 'remote' is the last entry on page 721. All words between 'remains' and 'remote' will appear on this page. Using the guide words can speed up your search.

** Using your knowledge about quartiles and guide words, see how quickly you can find these words in your dictionary.

repugnant	kappa
deluge	inconclusive
syllable	wattle

Understanding abbreviations and symbols

A dictionary relies on abbreviations and symbols in order to give as much information as possible in as small a space as possible.

Abbreviations

You don't need to spend time learning all the abbreviations. Be selective and concentrate on the most common ones and those which are of most use to you – for example, the parts of speech. You can always refer to the list of abbreviations as you need them.

Here are some common dictionary abbreviations.

Languages	
Du.	Dutch
Eng. or Engl.	English
Fr. or F.	French
Germ. or G.	German
Gr. or Gk.	Greek
Heb.	Hebrew
It.	Italian
L. or Lat.	Latin
M.E.	Middle English
O.E.	Old English
Sp.	Spanish

Parts of speech

adj. or a.	adjective
adv.	adverb
n.	noun
prep.	preposition
pron.	pronoun (can also mean pronunciation)
vb. or v.	verb

(v.t. verb transitive, v.i. verb intransitive)

Other abbreviations

abbrev. or abbr.	abbreviation
coll. or colloq.	colloquial
esp.	especially
exc.	except
irreg.	irregular
pa.t. or past t.	past tense
pfx. or pref.	prefix
pl.	plural
sing.	singular
sl.	slang
suff. or suf.	suffix
usu.	usually

You can see some of these abbreviations in use in the entry below.

fabric /ˈfæbrɪk/ *n.* **1 a** a woven material; a textile. **b** other material resembling woven cloth. **2** a structure or framework, esp. the walls, floor, and roof of a building. **3** (in abstract senses) the essential structure or essence of a thing (*the fabric of society*). [ME f. F *fabrique* f. L *fabrica* f. *faber* metal-worker etc.]

(from *The Concise Oxford Dictionary*)

Symbols

When you encounter a new word in your reading, you may be uncertain about its correct pronunciation. Check its pronunciation in your dictionary. Guidance on pronunciation will usually be given after each headword. The way it is presented will vary according to the dictionary you are using. It can appear:

within brackets or obliques after the entry;

fabulous /ˈfæbjʊləs/ *adj.* 1 incredible, exaggerated. absurd (*fabulous wealth*). 2 colloq. marvellous (*looking fabulous*). 3 a celebrated in fable. b legendary, mythical. □□ **fabulosity** /-ˈlɒsɪtɪ/ *n.* **fabulously** *adv.* **fabulousness** *n.* [F *fabuleux* or L *fabulosus* (as FABLE)]

(from *The Concise Oxford Dictionary*)

or in italics after the entry.

remove *ri-mōōv′*, *v.t.* to put or take away: to transfer: to withdraw: to displace: to make away with.—*v.i.* to go away: to change abode.—*n.* removal: step or degree of remoteness or indirectness: in some schools, an intermediate class.—*n.* **removabil′ity.**—*adj.* **remov′able.**—*adv.* **remov′ably.**—*n.* **remov′al** the act of taking away: displacing: change of place: transference: going away: change of abode: a euphemism for murder.—*adj.* **removed′** remote: distant by degrees, as in descent, relationship.—*ns.* **remov′edness; remov′er** one who or that which removes: one who conveys furniture from house to house. [O.Fr. *re-mouvoir*—L. *removēre*, *remōtum*—*re-*, away, *movēre*, to move.]

(from *Chambers Concise Dictionary*)

You may find the pronunciation symbols difficult to understand at first. The entry from the *Concise Oxford Dictionary* uses the IPA (International Phonetic Alphabet) to explain pronunciation. Most dictionaries use this system. Chambers dictionaries, which you may well find easier to follow, do not use phonetic symbols but a rough spelling guide instead.

Although the format of pronunciation guidance differs from one dictionary to another, all dictionaries indicate which part of a word should be emphasised. This emphasis is called stress. The way words are stressed is what gives our language its distinctive rhythm. A raised comma (') or an acute sign usually indicate which part of a word is stressed. In Chambers dictionaries the stressed syllable is the part of the word that occurs immediately before the sign, while in the *Concise Oxford Dictionary* the stressed syllable occurs immediately after the sign. You will need to check your own dictionary carefully so that you can interpret its symbols correctly.

** Look at the following words in your dictionary and, using the symbols, decide which syllable is stressed.

bizarre   primitive

harry   municipal

nibble   pompom

Understanding the terms

Parts of speech

To incorporate a word successfully into your natural vocabulary, you need to appreciate both its meaning and the way it is used in sentences. **By understanding the functions of the parts of speech, you will appreciate how to use new words correctly.** The parts of speech are:

nouns

adjectives

verbs

adverbs

pronouns

prepositions

All the parts of speech are contained within these two sentences:

Robin gently placed the sleepy puppy in a small oval basket by
the radiator. He carefully covered his pet with a light blanket.

A **noun** is a naming word used to name a person, place, animal or thing.

Robin, puppy, basket, radiator, pet, blanket are all nouns.

An **adjective** describes or gives more information about a noun.

sleepy puppy   small oval basket   light blanket

adjective noun   adjectives   noun   adjective noun

A **verb** expresses an action or a state of being.

placed   covered

verb   verb

An **adverb** gives more information about a verb – explaining when, how or where an action takes place. (At times it gives more information about an adjective or another adverb.)

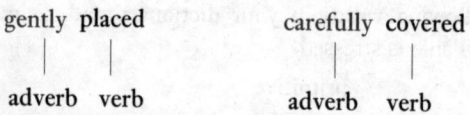

gently **placed**		carefully **covered**	
adverb	verb	adverb	verb

A **pronoun** is a word used instead of a noun. It refers to a thing or person previously mentioned.

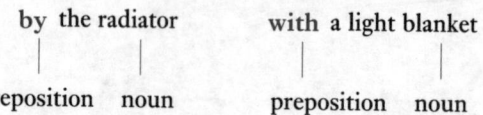

He

a pronoun used instead of the noun 'Robin'

A **preposition** usually introduces a phrase containing a noun or pronoun and shows the relationship between this noun or pronoun and another word in the sentence.

by **the radiator**		with **a light blanket**	
preposition	noun	preposition	noun

Knowing the part of speech of a new word will help you to use it more accurately. When you see or hear a new word, always try to remember or note down the sentence in which it was used so that you can work out its part of speech.

e.g. Erica loved to wear **voluminous** velvet dresses in dark colours.

You will work out that 'voluminous' describes the noun 'dresses' and so it is an **adjective**. Now check 'voluminous' in a dictionary. You will see that it is classified as an adjective: it is a word you will use to describe a noun.

Some words can act as more than one part of speech according to the way they are used in sentences. For example, the word 'ring' can be a noun or a verb.

ring   n.   a circle or small hoop

ring   v.i.   to give a metallic or bell-like sound

It is important to ensure that you are looking at the correct entry when you research a word.

** Look up these words in your dictionary. Notice the particular part of speech of each and then use each word in an interesting sentence.

cavernous furtively

collude caucus

ruminate

Using words in their contexts

If a word is marked coll./colloq. for colloquial or sl. for slang, it means it should be avoided in all formal writing and certain formal speaking situations. Colloquial words, even slang words, often form part of our everyday conversation and informal writing but we should always consider if our audience would find such words acceptable.

matey (maty) adj. (coll.) friendly or familiar

chomp v. (coll.) to munch with noisy enjoyment

grotty adj. (sl.) ugly, useless, unpleasant

bloke n. (sl.) a man

By now you will have a working knowledge of your dictionary.

You will appreciate how it can help you.

You will know where to find the lists of abbreviations and symbols and you will already be familiar with some of them.

You will be aware of how to find entries quickly and effectively.

You will appreciate the importance of understanding the various parts of speech.

You will now be ready to understand an entry and use your dictionary to research new words to make them part of your natural vocabulary.

In the next chapter you will examine entries in more detail. Dictionaries can be daunting and complicated to use, but if you understand how your dictionary is laid out and appreciate the terms, abbreviations and symbols used in it you can look up entries with confidence and your vocabulary will flourish.

3
Using Dictionaries

Understanding entries

In the last chapter you saw how important it is to familiarise yourself with the layout of your dictionary and the format of an entry.

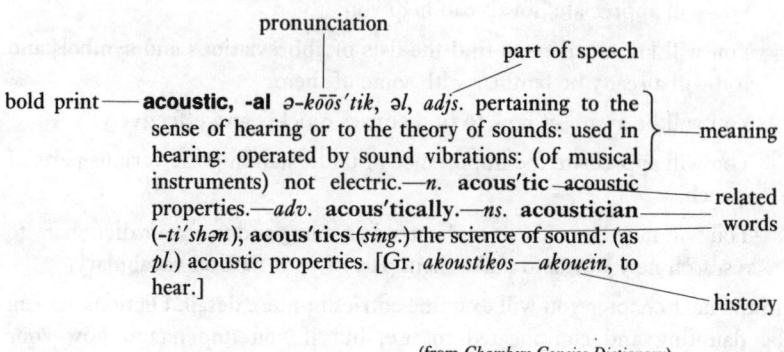

(from *Chambers Concise Dictionary*)

bold print

This is used not only for the headword itself but all the words related to the headword. It allows us to locate the word we need.

pronunciation (*ə-kōōs'tik, -əl*)

There is a guide to the word's pronunciation immediately after the headword. It divides the word into syllables and shows how the vowels and consonants should be pronounced and which part of the word should be stressed.

In 'acoustic',

the initial vowel is neutral and has no very definite vowel value

the 'ou' is pronounced as a long 'ōō' sound

'c' in each position has a hard 'k' sound

the second syllable 'kōōs' is stressed

It is important to understand the signs and symbols for pronunciation because in order to absorb new words into your vocabulary you need both to pronounce and use them in an acceptable way.

part of speech

Next comes the abbreviation for the part of speech. 'Acoustic' is an adjective. It is mentioned in the plural as the two adjectives 'acoustic' and 'acoustical' are shown.

meaning

The main part of the entry is taken up by the definition.

> pertaining to the sense of hearing or to the theory of sounds: used in hearing: operated by sound vibrations: (of musical instruments) not electric
>
> (from *Chambers Concise Dictionary*)

Notice how each part of the explanation is separated from the next by a colon.

A definition can be difficult to understand because:

▸ It may contain other unfamiliar words within the explanation. If this is so then follow up the unfamiliar word. (In this case it may be necessary to look up 'pertaining' – belonging to or relating to.)

▸ The entry may be a complicated word which is difficult to explain in simple terms.

▸ The word may concern a subject which we have little knowledge about.

related words

Each related word appears in bold type and is treated in a similar manner: part of speech; the word; sometimes additional advice about pronunciation; meaning. Each related word is separated from the next by a long hyphen.

> — n. **acoustic** – acoustic properties. – adv. **acoustically**. — ns. **acoustician** (-ti'-sh n): **acoustics** (sing.) the science of sound: (as pl.) acoustic properties

history

An explanation of the word's origins appears in square brackets at the end of each entry; any additional information is given in round brackets within the square brackets. Here 'acoustic' comes from the Greek word *akoustikos*, from *akouien*, to hear.

Here is another entry for the same word.

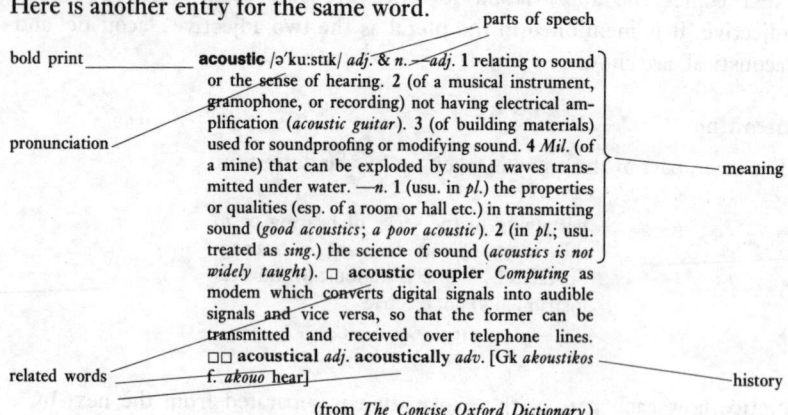

(from *The Concise Oxford Dictionary*)

You will notice that, although the format is similar, there are some differences.

similarities

▶ The headword is in bold type.

▶ The same abbreviations are used for the parts of speech and they are placed before the word they directly refer to. This entry also shows adj. & n. together, indicating the two functions of the word before dealing with each individually. This is not present in the previous entry.

▶ The history of the word is given in square brackets at the end.

differences

▶ Although the pronunciation guide appears after the headword, it is contained within obliques and uses the symbols of the International Phonetic Alphabet.

▶ The sign for the stressed syllable is placed before the syllable that is stressed ('ku'); in the Chambers entry it is placed after the stressed syllable.

▶ The meanings are numbered with the most familiar and important meaning given first.

If you are using a different dictionary, examine the entry for 'acoustic' in your own dictionary to see how it differs from the two entries given here. Dictionaries are frequently revised and updated so the layout in your dictionary could well be different.

With practice you will soon become familiar with the format of the entries in your dictionary.

** Look up the entry for each of these words. Study each carefully and notice how each entry has a similar layout. (Don't forget to follow up any unfamiliar words that appear within a definition.)

parasite	jade	exempt
puce	tetchy	cordon bleu

Understanding meaning

People often complain that it is difficult to find out the exact meaning of a word as dictionary definitions are hard to understand. When you compared the two entries for 'acoustic', you may have preferred one of the dictionary's definitions to the other. It is a matter of personal taste and you may look up another word and find the reverse is true – there is no perfect dictionary.

It is sometimes beneficial to consult more than one concise dictionary so that you can consider the different ways of expressing a definition.

'Translating' the definition

When you look up the meaning of a word, don't try to remember the exact dictionary definition; recalling the precise definition is difficult and often unhelpful. 'Translate' the definition into your own words. This will help you to understand, remember and feel comfortable with the word. If you don't fully understand the definition, you won't be able to use the word. For example, **'acoustic'** may be summed up in your own terms like this: 'it has something to do with sound or the sense of hearing'. Record your definition in your personal dictionary then use the word in several sentences so that you become accustomed to it.

EXAMPLES:

The acoustics in the new concert hall are perfect.

noun (pl) (meaning: sound qualities)

The acoustic matting in the ward helped to deaden the sound of the nurse's footsteps.

adjective (meaning: designed to absorb sound)

The study of acoustics is a part of the physics syllabus.

noun (sing) (meaning: the science of sound)

Different meanings

When you research a word, you may find it has more than one meaning.

e.g.

> shanty[1] *shant'i, n.* a roughly built hut: a ramshackle dwelling: a low public-house. —**shanty town** a town, or an area of one, where housing is makeshift and ramshackle. [Perh. Fr. *chantier*, a timber-yard (in Canada a woodcutters' headquarters); perh. Ir. *sean tig*, old house.]
> shanty[2] *shan'ti, n.* a song with chorus, sung by sailors while heaving at the capstan, or the like —also **chanty, chantie, chantey** (*shan'ti*). —*n.* **shant'yman** the solo-singer in shanties. [Said to be from Fr. *chantezc* imper.), sing.]
>
> (from *Chambers Concise Dictionary*)

Always check each entry to ensure you are researching the correct entry for your situation.

** Look up the meanings of these words in your dictionary. 'Translate' each definition into your own language and record an entry for each in your personal dictionary.

taint (used as a verb)	eddy (noun)
manacle (noun)	mellow (adjective)
exodus (noun)	exhume (verb)
donor (noun)	gregarious (adjective)
nonchalant (adjective)	deign (verb)

An entry frequently offers you shades of meaning. It is important to consider all the options and not merely choose the first words in the explanation. You usually only look up words you have heard or read, so recall the way in which they were used so that you can check that you have chosen the correct shade of meaning.

e.g. Her stooped frame and shaking hands <u>belied</u> her <u>acute</u> intellect.

belie *bi'li*, *v.t.* to give the lie to: to speak falsely of: to present in a false character: to counterfeit: to be false to: to falsify: to fail to fulfil or justify: – *pr.p.* bely'ing; *pa.t.* and *pa.p.* belied'. [be- (3).]

acute a'kut, adj. sharp: sharp-pointed: keen: piercing: finely discriminating: shrewd: urgently pressing: of a disease, coming to a crisis, as opp. to chronic. – n. an acute accent. – adv. acute'ly. – n. acute'ness. – acute accent a mark (') over letters, used for various purposes: acute angle one less than a right angle. [L. acutus. pa.p. of acuere, to sharpen.]

(from *Chambers Concise Dictionary*)

3

You have to select the meaning that is correct for you in this instance. For **belied** you might choose 'gave the lie to' as the definition which best fits this context.

For **acute**, the terms 'sharp', 'keen', 'finely discriminating' or 'shrewd' could be used to describe her mind, whilst 'sharp-pointed', 'urgently pressing' or 'of a disease coming to crisis' are inappropriate.

Researching words

It is useful to develop a procedure for new words. You were introduced to this idea in Chapter 1. If possible, note down the sentence in which you heard or saw the word.

Guessing

▶ See if you can guess the meaning from the context it is used in.

▶ Does it look like another word you know? e.g. If you were researching 'revere', it may remind you of 'reverend' or 'reverence' and help you to work out its meaning.

▶ Which part of speech is this word?

Use your dictionary

▶ Look carefully at all the meanings or shades of meaning in the dictionary entry.

▶ If the definition contains any words you are uncertain about, check the meaning of these.

▶ Select the meaning appropriate for your situation.

▶ Translate the definition into your own words.

▶ Does this definition make sense in your sentence?

Pronunciation

Check you are pronouncing the word correctly and putting the stress on the right syllable.

Are there alternative ways of pronouncing it?

Part of speech

Note its part of speech.

Spelling

Learn how to spell the word:

copy the word

notice and underline any difficult parts

cover the word

write it from memory

check

If you have made a mistake, start again. It is worth spending some time doing this as you will not be able to make full use of a word in your writing unless you are confident about its spelling.

Are there alternative ways of spelling the word? e.g. **icon, ikon n.** (a sacred image, statue, painting or mosaic – perhaps of a sacred person)

Are there any changes to the spelling? e.g. **propel v.** (to drive forward) propelling, prope_ll_ed, prope_ll_ant, prope_ll_er

Related words

If you have time, look at the words derived from the headword and note down any words which will be useful to you.

Origins

If you are interested in words, find out where the word came from. Such knowledge can sometimes help you to unlock the meaning of other words from the same root.

Recording your findings

In Chapter 1 you were introduced to the idea of developing a personal dictionary.

Always note down:

the meaning or meanings – expressed in your own words

the part of speech

You may decide that you want to record more details, for example a **sentence or sentences containing the word**, or help with **spelling** (e.g. if part of a word appears difficult to remember then either underline or write that part in a different colour), or **synonyms**. If you have time, research your new word further by using a thesaurus.

e.g. Researching the word 'apprehension'.

What sentence did it occur in?

His earlier self-confidence gave way to **apprehension** as he looked through his binoculars at the sheer rock face that lay ahead.

The dictionary definition

> *n.* **apprehension** act of apprehending or seizing: arrest:
> conscious perception: conception: ability to understand: fear

(from Chambers Concise Dictionary)

Your personal dictionary entry

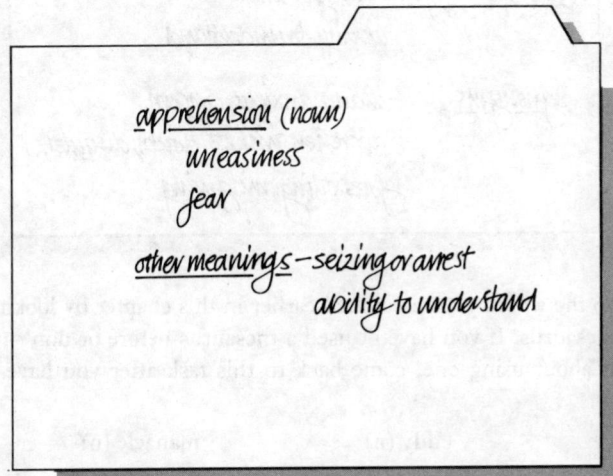

apprehension (noun)
uneasiness
fear

other meanings – seizing or arrest
ability to understand

The thesaurus definition

Now look up 'apprehension' in your thesaurus and note down all the appropriate words associated with fear so that you can enter them into your personal dictionary.

apprehension 1. alarm, anxiety, apprehensiveness, concern, disquiet, doubt, dread, fear, foreboding, misgiving, mistrust, premonition, suspicion, unease, uneasiness, worry **2.** arrest, capture, catching, seizure, taking **3.** awareness, comprehension, grasp, intellect, intelligence, ken, knowledge, perception, understanding **4.** belief, concept, conception, conjecture, idea, impression, notion, opinion, sentiment, thought, view

(from *Collins Paperback Thesaurus*)

The final entry in your personal dictionary

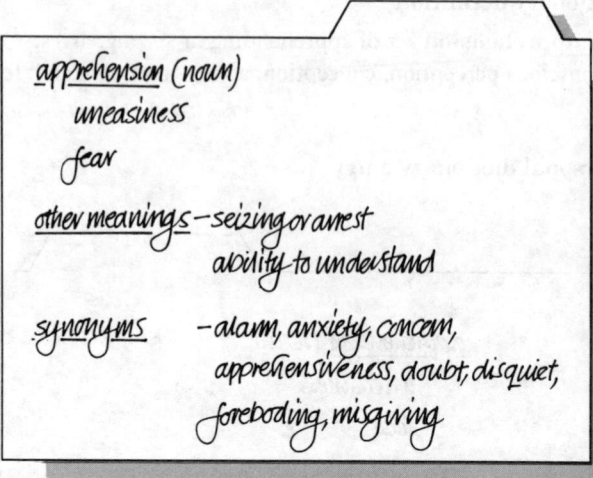

apprehension (noun)
uneasiness
fear

other meanings – seizing or arrest
ability to understand

synonyms – alarm, anxiety, concern, apprehensiveness, doubt, disquiet, foreboding, misgiving

** Follow up the words you researched earlier in this chapter by looking them up in a thesaurus. If you haven't used a thesaurus before or don't feel very confident about using one, come back to this task after you have studied Chapter 4.

taint (v)   eddy (n)   manacle (n)

mellow (adj)   exodus (n)   exhume (v)

gregarious (adj)   nonchalant (adj)   deign (v)

Having researched these words in both a dictionary and thesaurus, you should feel much happier about their meanings and feel confident about using them in sentences.

** Use each word in an interesting sentence.

Final thoughts

For every word you research,

look it up in your dictionary,

enter your findings in your personal dictionary,

use the word in a sentence immediately,

find synonyms in your thesaurus,

use the new word as much as possible in your writing
and conversation

and the word will become a part of your natural
vocabulary.

You may feel that researching a new word is a laborious and lengthy process. At first, writing each entry in your personal dictionary may take you a considerable time, but as you gain confidence and are more effective at using a dictionary and thesaurus, you will become more efficient.

** Read this short descriptive passage from Iris Murdoch's *The Philosopher's Son*. Use your dictionary to research the underlined words.

> It was raining hard. The <u>malignant</u> rain rattled on the car
> like shot. Propelled in <u>oblique</u> <u>flurries</u>, it <u>assaulted</u> the
> windscreen, <u>obliterating</u> in a second the <u>frenetic</u> strivings of
> the windscreen wipers. Little demonic faces composed of
> racing raindrops appeared and vanished. The intermittent
> yellow light of the street lamps, illuminating the grey <u>atoms</u>
> of the storm, <u>fractured</u> in sudden stars upon the rain-
> swarmed glass. Bumping on cobbles the car hummed and
> drummed.

When you have completed Chapter 4, come back to this task and, using your thesaurus, see if you can find alternative and appropriate replacement words.

If you want to improve and enlarge your natural vocabulary, time and effort are needed. The pleasure and confidence you gain as your vocabulary increases will amply reward you.

4
Using a Thesaurus

What is a thesaurus?

If you refer to a dictionary to find the meaning of the word 'thesaurus', you will find it defined as 'a treasury or a storehouse of knowledge'. However, today the word is most often used for **a book containing a collection of synonyms, related words and antonyms.**

Synonyms are words which have a similar meaning to each other.

EXAMPLES:

    mend – fix, restore, heal, rectify.

    top – apex, pinnacle, crest, head.

Remember, synonyms have similar meanings but not necessarily <u>the same</u> meaning. You must carefully consider how a word is being used in a sentence before replacing it with a synonym.

e.g. The lawn mower was very reliable after it was <u>mended</u>. ✓

    The lawn mower was very reliable after it was <u>healed</u>. ✗

Antonyms are words which have the opposite meaning to each other.

e.g. <u>nervous</u>: confident, calm, equable, bold

As with synonyms, a list of antonyms will reflect shades of meaning.

There are different types of thesauruses (some are called dictionaries of synonyms and antonyms) but these shouldn't be confused with general English dictionaries. They fulfil the same function as a thesaurus – listing synonyms and antonyms but rarely giving definitions.

destroy *vb.* 1 ruin, demolish; deface, spoil: *These trees were destroyed by disease.* 2 kill, slay, end, extinguish: *When I saw the train pulling out of the station, my holiday plans were destroyed.* ANT. (1) create, start, undertake.

destruction *n.* devastation, demolition, ruin, extinction. ANT. creation, beginning. — synonyms

part of speech —

detach *vb.* separate, disengage, divide. ANT. attach, connect.

detail *n.* feature, aspect; item, circumstance.

detain *vb.* delay, restrain, hold back, stop. ANT. forward, hurry, rush.

antonyms listed after ANT

detect *vb.* determine, discover, ascertain, learn, find out.

detective *n.* policeman, officer.

deter *vb.* prevent, discourage, dissuade. ANT. encourage.

deteriorate *vb.* decay, degenerate, decline; impair; disintegrate. ANT. improve.

determine *vb.* 1 decide, settle, resolve: *It was only a few minutes to determine who had eaten the sweets – he had chocolate all over his chin.* 2 fix, establish, define: *I wasn't able to determine exactly where my property ended and my neighbour's began.*

synonyms for the two meanings of 'determine' shown with example sentences

(from *The Dictionary of Synonyms and Antonyms*)

In general, a thesaurus will give more examples of related and contrasting words than a dictionary of synonyms and antonyms, but the difference between the two is often difficult to see. For ease, we will refer to all books of synonyms as thesauruses.

Types of thesauruses

Alphabetical arrangement

These follow the same arrangement as standard English dictionaries with guide words at the top of each page and the headword for each entry given in bold type. As some headwords will have several distinct meanings, the synonyms are usually grouped according to the variations in meaning. To use this type of thesaurus, follow the procedure for using a dictionary.

emporium

emporium bazaar, market, mart, shop, store

empower allow, authorize, commission, delegate, enable, entitle, license, permit, qualify, sanction, warrant

emptiness 1. bareness, blankness, desertedness, desolation, destitution, vacancy, vacuum, void, waste **2.** aimlessness, banality, barrenness, frivolity, futility, hollowness, inanity, ineffectiveness, meaninglessness, purposelessness, senselessness, silliness, unreality, unsatisfactoriness, unsubstantiality, vainness, valuelessness, vanity, worthlessness **3.** cheapness, hollowness, idleness, insincerity, triviality, trivialness **4.** absentness, blankness, expressionlessness, unintelligence, vacancy, vacantness, vacuity, vacuousness **5.** *Inf.* desire, hunger, ravening

empty *adj.* **1.** ~~bare, blank,~~ clear, deserted, desolate, destitute, hollow, unfurnished, uninhabited, unoccupied, untenanted, vacant, void, waste **2.** aimless, banal, bootless, frivolous, fruitless, futile, hollow, inane, ineffective, meaningless, purposeless, senseless, silly, unreal, unsatisfactory, unsubstantial, vain, valueless, worthless **3.** cheap, hollow, idle, insincere, trivial **4.** absent, blank, expressionless, unintelligent, vacant, vacuous **5.** *Inf.* famished, hungry, ravenous, starving (*Inf.*), unfed, unfilled *v.* **6.** clear, consume, deplete, discharge, drain, dump, evacuate, exhaust, gut, pour out, unburden, unload, use up, vacate, void

empty-headed brainless, dizzy (*Inf.*), featherbrained, flighty, frivolous, giddy, harebrained, inane, scatterbrained, silly, skittish, vacuous

enable allow, authorize, capacitate, commission, empower, facilitate, fit, license, permit, prepare qualify, sanction, warrant

enact 1. authorize, command, decree, establish, legislate, ordain, order, pass, proclaim, ratify, sanction **2.** act, act out, appear as, depict, perform, personate, play, play the part of, portray, represent

enactment 1. authorization, command, commandment, decree, dictate, edict, law, legislation, order, ordinance, proclamation, ratification, regulation, statute **2.** acting, depiction, performance, personation, play-acting, playing, portrayal, representation

enamour bewitch, captivate, charm, enchant, endear, enrapture, entrance, fascinate, infatuate.

enamoured bewitched, captivated, charmed, crazy about (*Inf.*), enchanted, enraptured entranced, fascinated, fond, infatuated, in love, nuts on ~~or about~~ (*Sl.*), smitten, swept off one's feet, taken, wild about (*Inf.*)

(from *The Collins Paperback Thesaurus*)

Entries for antonyms are usually more brief and occur either:

after the list of synonyms for each entry (as shown in the first extract in this chapter) or

at the end of the book in a separate section (as shown below).

N

naive artful, disingenuous, sly, sophisticated

narrow ample, big, broad, broad-minded, generous, liberal, open, receptive, spacious, wide

nasty admirable, clean, decent, enjoyable, kind, nice, pleasant, sweet

natural affected, artificial, assumed, counterfeit, feigned, unnatural

neat awful, bad, cluttered, disorderly, disorganized, incompetent, inefficient, messy, terrible, untidy

necessary dispensable, non-essential, unnecessary

needless beneficial, essential, obligatory, required, useful

nefarious admirable, good, honest, honourable, just, noble, praiseworthy

negative affirmative, approving, assenting, cheerful, concurring, optimistic, positive

neglect *v.* appreciate, attend to, notice, observe, regard, remember, value ~*n.* attention, care, consideration, notice, regard, respect

negligent attentive, careful, considerate, mindful, rigorous, thoughtful

nervous bold, calm, confident, constant, equable, even, peaceful, steady

neutral active, belligerent, biased, decided, interested, interfering, partial, participating, positive

new aged, ancient, antique, experienced, hackneyed, old, old-fashioned, outmoded, stale, trite

nice awful, careless, coarse, crude, disagreeable, dreadful, ill-bred, mean, rough, shabby, sloppy, miserable, unfriendly, unkind, unpleasant, vague, vulgar

nicely carelessly, sloppily, unattractively, unfortunately, unpleasantly

niggardly abundant, ample, bountiful, copious, generous, handsome, lavish, liberal, munificent, plentiful, profuse.

nimble awkward, clumsy, dull, heavy, inactive, indolent, lethargic, slow

noble *n.* commoner, peasant, serf ~*adj.* base, contemptible, despicable, dishonest, humble, ignoble, insignificant, lowborn, lowly, mean, modest, peasant, plain, plebian, selfish, vulgar.

noisy hushed, quiet, silent, still, subdued, tuneful

nondescript distinctive, extraordinary, unique unusual

nonessential appropriate, essential, important, significant, vital

nonsense fact, reality, reason, sense, seriousness, truth, wisdom

normal abnormal, exceptional, irregular, peculiar, rare, remarkable, singular, uncommon, unnatural, unusual

notable anonymous, concealed, hidden, imperceptible, obscure, unknown, vague

noted infamous, obscure, undistinguished, unknown

notice *v.* disregard, ignore, neglect, overlook ~*n.* disregard, ignorance, omission, oversight, neglect

novel ancient, common, customary, familiar, habitual, old-fashioned, ordinary, run-of-the-mill, traditional, usual

novice master, old hand, professional, teacher

nuisance benefit, blessing, delight, happiness, joy, pleasure, satisfaction

number *n.* insufficiency, lack, scantiness, scarcity, shortage, want ~*v.* conjecture, guess, mass, theorize

numerous few, not many, scarcely any

nurture deprive, disregard, ignore, neglect, overlook

(from *The Collins Paperback Thesaurus*)

Roget's Thesaurus

Whilst we wouldn't recommend buying this type of thesaurus (see below), there may be occasions when you need to consult one.

Thesauruses based on Dr Roget's original version, written in the 19th century, are published by several companies. They follow his original format but the words and page layout have been updated.

These types of thesauruses aim to provide 'suitable words to express an idea clearly and concisely'. They are not only concerned with providing synonyms but also with giving a variety of related words and phrases ranging from formal language to slang.

4

400 Loudness

N. *loudness*, distinctness, audibility 398 *sound*; noise, loud n., ear-splitting n; high volume; broken silence, shattered s., knock, knocking; burst of sound, report, loud r., sonic boom, slam, clap, thunderclap, burst, shell b., explosion 402 *bang*; siren, alarm, honk, toot 665 *danger signal;* prolonged noise, reverberation, plangency, boom, rattle 403 *roll*; thunder, rattling t., war in heaven 176 *storm*; dashing, surging, hissing 406 *sibilation*; fire, gunfire, artillery, blitz 712 *bombardment*; stridency, brassiness, shrillness, blast, blare, bray, fanfare, flourish 407 *stridor*; trumpet blast, clarion call, view halloo 547 *call*; sonority, organ notes, clang, clangour 404 *resonance*; ringing tones; bells, peal, chimes 412 *campanology*; diapason, swell, crescendo, fortissimo, tutti, full blast, full chorus; vociferation, clamour, outcry, roaring, shouting, bawling, yelling, screaming, whoop, shout, howl, shriek, scream, roar 408 *cry*, 409 *ululation*; loud laughter, cachinnation 835 *laughter* loud breathing, stertorousness 352 *respiration*; noisiness, din, row, deafening r., racket, crash, clash, clatter, hubbub, hullabaloo, ballyhoo, song and dance, slamming, banging, stamping, chanting, hooting, uproar, stramash, shemozzle, tumult, bedlam, pandemonium, all hell let loose 61 *turmoil.*

megaphone, amplifier, loud pedal; public address system, loudhailer, loudspeaker, speaker, microphone, mike; ear trumpet 415 *hearing aid*; loud instrument, whistle, siren, hooter, horn, klaxon, gong; rattle, bullroarer; buzzer, bell, alarm, door knocker; trumpet, brass; ghetto blaster; stentorian voice, lungs, good l., good pair of l., lungs of brass, iron throat; Stentor, town crier.

Adj. *loud*, distinct, audible, heard; turned right up, at full volume, at full pitch, at the top of one's voice; noisy, full of noise, rackety, uproarious, rowdy, rumbustious 61 *disorderly*; multisonous, many-tongued 411 *discordant*; clamorous, clamant, shouting, yelling, whooping, screaming, bellowing 408 *crying*; big- mouthed, loud-m.; sonorous, booming, deep, full, powerful; lusty, full-throated, stentorian, brazen-mouthed, trumpet-tongued; ringing, carrying; deafening, dinning; piercing, ear-splitting, ear-rending; thundering, thunderous, rattling, crashing; pealing, clangorous, plangent; shrill, high-sounding 407 *strident*; blaring, brassy; echoing, resounding 404 *resonant*; swelling, crescendo; fortissimo, enough to waken the dead.

Vb. *be loud*, – noisy etc. adj.; break the silence; speak up, give tongue, raise the voice, strain one's v.; call, catcall, caterwaul; skirl, scream, whistle 407 *shrill*; vociferate, shout 408 *cry*; cachinnate 835 *laugh*; clap, stamp, raise the roof, raise the rafters; roar, bellow, howl 409 *ululate*; din, sound, boom, reverberate 404 *resound*; rattle, thunder, fulminate, storm, clash; ring, peal, clang, crash; bray, blare; slam 402 *bang*; burst, explode, detonate, go off; knock, knock hard, hammer, drill; deafen, stun; split the ears, rend the eardrums, shatter the e., ring in the ear; swell, fill the air; rend the skies, make the welkin ring, rattle the windows, awake the echoes, waken the dead; raise Cain, kick up a shindy, make the devil of a row 61 *rampage.*

Adv. *loudly*, distinctly etc. adj.; noisily, dinningly; aloud, at the top of one's voice, lustily; in full cry, full blast, full chorus; fortissimo, crescendo.

(from The Original Roget's Thesaurus of English Words and Phrases)

The main part of *Roget's Thesaurus* is divided into six sections.

Abstract Relations	Intellect
Space	Volition
Matter	Emotion, Religion, Morality

Word lists are arranged under further sub-divisions within these main classes. Obviously such an arrangement means that most users have to refer to the index to find the required entry. The index of keywords is arranged in alphabetical order at the end of the book.

To use *Roget's Thesaurus*, follow these steps.

Consider the idea or word you wish to express or replace.

Refer to the index to see if it is listed.

Yes

No

Consider the various aspects listed — the keywords.

Find an alternative way of expressing the word or idea.

Select the keyword most closely related to your word or idea.

Refer to section number given for this keyword.

Locate synonyms for the keyword.

Helpful Hints

▶ Carefully consider the various alternative keywords listed in the index. It can be difficult to make the correct choice, so be prepared to go back to the index to select another keyword if you have made the wrong choice.

e.g. blunt

> *i.e.* blunt *weaken* 163vb.
> *inert* 175 adj.
> *moderate* 177 vb.
> *low* 210 adj.
> *unsharpened* 257 adj.
> *blunt* 257 vb.
> *smooth* 258 adj.
> *render insensible* 375 vb.
> *undisguised* 522 adj.
> *assertive* 532 adj.
> *veracious* 540 adj.
> *artless* 699 adj.
> *dibs* 797 n.
> *make insensitive* 820 vb.
> *ill-bred* 847 adj.
> *ungracious* 885 adj.

(from *The Original Roget's Thesaurus of English Words and Phrases*)

If you wanted to find another word to describe a blunt pencil, you would probably choose the keywords 'blunt' or 'unsharpened'. Both are found under section 257. However, if you wanted to describe someone whose manner was blunt, you might choose the keyword 'ill-bred' and refer to section 847, or 'ungracious' in section 885.

▶ Even though Roget's Thesaurus has been updated, some of the listed words are obscure.

e.g. vehicle – palanquin

▶ Slang and colloquial words are not identified as such but it is important to avoid such words in formal writing and speech.

** Using a thesaurus, and a dictionary where necessary, find suitable synonyms for each of the words underlined in these sentences.

1 The child was <u>reprimanded</u> by his parents.

2 It is <u>expected</u> that inflation will start to <u>fall</u> by the autumn.

3 The <u>shiny</u> green leaves provided a good contrast to the <u>bright</u> flowers.

4 Her writing was very <u>neat</u>.

5 The match was long and <u>boring</u>; most of the spectators had left before the final whistle.

6 I <u>am sorry</u> to <u>inform</u> you that you were unsuccessful on this occasion.

** Use your thesaurus to find antonyms for these words.

lucky	heroic	clever	begin
bitter	grow	reluctant	hesitant

Choosing a thesaurus

In Chapter 2 you were advised to look at a number of dictionaries before buying one; it is sensible to follow the same procedure before choosing a thesaurus. You may need to consider whether you will always use a thesaurus in one place or if you will need to carry it around with you. Like dictionaries, thesauruses come in a range of sizes – from pocket books to large volumes of over a thousand pages. Generally the standard paperback version is adequate, reasonably priced and of a sensible size.

Although a thesaurus based on Dr Roget's original version will probably contain more words, you will undoubtedly find that a straightforward alphabetical arrangement is easier to use and more relevant to your needs.

You should also look at the date of the edition as, if that edition was printed some years ago, it may contain outdated and obscure words which may make selection a chore. The latest editions tend to be more clearly laid out and easier to follow.

When you have chosen your thesaurus, take time to familiarise yourself with its arrangement and features. You will need to read the introduction and refer to the list of abbreviations so that you are able to understand entries fully and extract as much information as possible from them.

You may find it helpful to look at these thesauruses before deciding which to buy.

> *The Collins Paperback Thesaurus in A–Z Form*
> *The Oxford Study Thesaurus*
> *Chambers Dictionary of Synonyms and Antonyms*
> *Collins Pocket Thesaurus in A–Z form*

Dictionaries versus thesauruses

You may consider that it is only necessary to have either a dictionary or a thesaurus but they are complementary and fulfil different functions. If you are serious about acquiring a more extensive vocabulary, you need both.

When Dr Roget was compiling his thesaurus, he believed that no definitions of synonyms were required as the reader would automatically select the most appropriate word. Other thesauruses have followed his example. However, he was probably rather optimistic about the extent of the user's vocabulary – most of us need to check precise meanings in a dictionary. Look back to the Roget entry for *loudness*. You will probably find several unfamiliar words which you need to research in a dictionary.

A dictionary will sometimes provide several synonyms for a headword.

> **happy** [*hapi*] *adj.* feeling or expressing joy, glad; pleased, contented; causing joy, gladness or pleasure; lucky, fortunate; successful; apt, appropriate; (*coll*) tipsy ~ happily *adv* ~ happiness *n*.
>
> (from *Penguin English Dictionary*)

However, if you look up the same word in a thesaurus a greater number of synonyms will be given. This wealth of choice enables you to select the exact word you require.

> **happy** 1. blessed, blest, blissful, blithe, cheerful, content, contented, delighted, ecstatic, elated, glad, gratified, jolly, joyful, joyous, jubilant, merry, overjoyed, over the moon (*Inf.*), pleased, sunny, thrilled, walking on air (*Inf.*) 2. advantageous, appropriate, apt, auspicious, befitting, convenient, enviable, favourable, felicitous, fortunate, lucky, opportune, promising, propitious, satisfactory, seasonable, successful, timely, well-timed
>
> (from *The Collins Paperback Thesaurus in A–Z form*)

By using a dictionary in conjunction with a thesaurus, you will avoid making mistakes and find you can research words more effectively.

If you haven't already attempted the exercise on page 38, you should now feel sufficiently confident to tackle it.

When to use a thesaurus

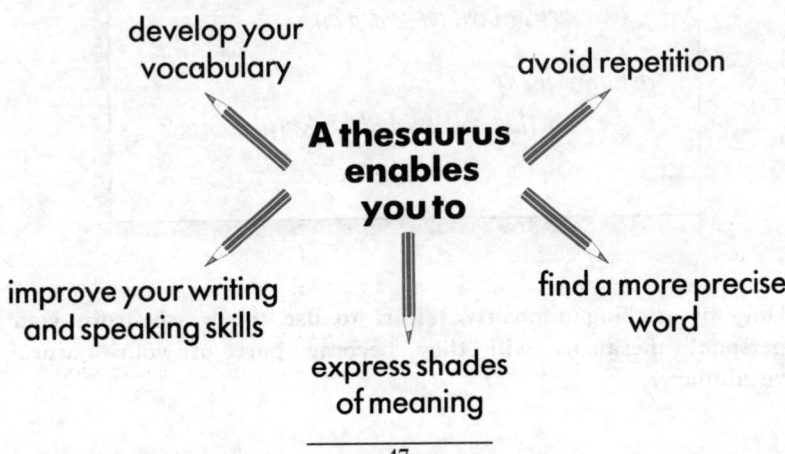

develop your vocabulary

avoid repetition

A thesaurus enables you to

improve your writing and speaking skills

express shades of meaning

find a more precise word

To develop your vocabulary

Most of us want to extend our vocabularies – to acquire and use a greater variety of words. A thesaurus is an important tool in this process. It can be used in two ways.

▶ By 'dipping in' and considering the variety and range of synonyms, you will increase your awareness and appreciation of words. You may find an interesting word that prompts you to refer to a dictionary to find its exact meaning.

▶ You may prefer to use the thesaurus for specific words. You have already thought about your vocabulary and how it can be improved, and have identified words that you overuse or use imprecisely. By referring to a thesaurus to find alternatives for these words, you will be consciously extending your vocabulary.

In Chapters 1 and 3 you considered developing your own personal dictionary. You may decide to include synonyms for each entry, compiling a joint personal dictionary and thesaurus. Or you may prefer to develop each separately. By using a separate card index system for your personal thesaurus you will be able to record more detailed information: usage, alternative spelling, example sentences, etc.

> use (verb)
> operate (machinery)
> utilise (or utilize) – suggest 'usefulness'
>   e.g. We utilised the remaining spare parts
>   when we built the second bike.
>
> consume – use up
>   e.g. They consumed all the food in the house.

Only by making a positive effort to use the words from your personal thesaurus will they become part of your natural vocabulary.

To improve your writing and speaking skills

Whether you are planning a formal speech, or writing a letter, report or essay, it is advisable to refer to your thesaurus after you have written the first draft. Get your ideas down on paper before considering how your writing can be improved. Then read through the draft and, as part of your check, underline any words that appear repetitive, imprecise, inappropriate or dull. Refer to your thesaurus for suitable alternatives.

Helpful Hints

4

▶ You may be presented with many alternatives but only some will be suitable for the given situation.

▶ Check the meaning of any unfamiliar words in a dictionary.

▶ The most appropriate word will often be the simplest and most direct word – consider your audience.

▶ You may need to rephrase your sentence after substituting a new word or words.

e.g. He spoke well.

He was articulate.

** Read through the draft letter of complaint shown overleaf. You may find some of the underlined words acceptable, or feel others need replacing. Look at the lists of synonyms below and select the word you consider would be most effective in each instance.

want – wish, desire, need

protest – object, complain, remonstrate

got – achieved, acquired, obtained, bought

components – elements, constituents, ingredients

says – announces, mentions, speaks, states, declares

has – possesses, comprises, contains, embodies, includes

think – believe, conclude, estimate, imagine, surmise

normally – commonly, habitually, regularly, usually

return – revert, repay, restore, recompense, refund

> 12 Ford Road,
> Perry Wood,
> Birmingham.
> B23 6YT
>
> Complaints Manager,
> United Chocolates plc,
> PO Box 45,
> Leeds.
> LD4 5TJ
>
> 23 May 1992
>
> Dear Sir,
>
> I _want_ to _protest_ about the Choc-o-delight bar which I _got_ _from_ Tresbury's in Chichester on 21st May.
>
> The list of _components_ on the wrapper _says_ that the bar _has_ nuts and raisins. The bar I bought contained just one nut and one raisin. _I think_ these bars _normally_ contain more nuts and raisins.
>
> As I am _unhappy_ with this purchase, I would like you to _return_ my money.
>
> Yours faithfully,
>
> V. Downes (Mrs)

Final thoughts

▶ An alphabetically arranged thesaurus is easier to use.

▶ A thesaurus and dictionary can help you to use:

   a more precise word;

   a more interesting word;

   a greater variety of words.

▶ Beware of becoming verbose – continue to use simple and direct words to express your ideas; **make clarity and precision your prime aims.**

5

Reading and Vocabulary

Reading is an integral part of our everyday lives; we are continually bombarded with the printed word in the form of

letters

notices

advertisements

instructions

newspapers

magazines

books

There is a clear relationship between reading and vocabulary. As Chapter 1 suggested, there is a number of ways to improve vocabulary, but reading is probably the most effective method and for many people the most enjoyable.

Helpful Hints

To extend your vocabulary by reading you should:

▶ read from a wide variety of sources

▶ read sufficiently demanding material

▶ mark or note down words which are unfamiliar

▶ research these words

▶ enter them in a personal dictionary

▶ practise using them

In this chapter we will consider:

how we read

the **different types of reading skills** we need

the **difficulties** we may encounter when reading

What is reading?

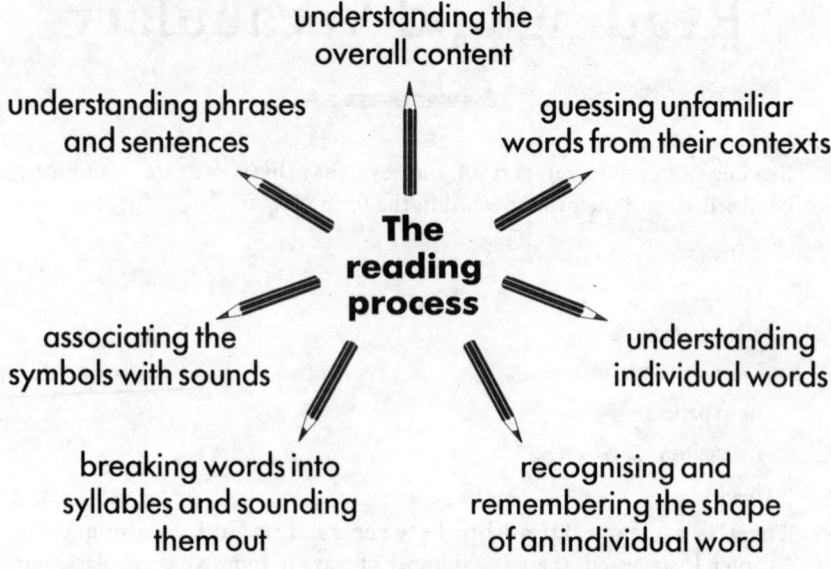

As adults we have reached a sophisticated stage of reading but we will all have passed through certain processes. Although we may have learnt by different methods, at some time everyone will have looked at a word and read that word by remembering its overall shape. At a later stage we learnt to associate symbols with sounds. Once that skill was developed, it was possible to read unfamiliar regular words by sounding them out. As English is not a phonetically regular language, we still have to use our ability to see an overall shape of a word in order to read those words that cannot be sounded out. Although we started the reading process by learning individual words, we soon graduated to phrases and sentences. At first our reading was slow and deliberate as we struggled with the mechanics of the task; comprehension developed at a later stage as we became more familiar with the reading of a wider variety of words.

Even as adults, if we read a text with too many unfamiliar words we read more slowly and fail to extract the full meaning from it. We must understand the majority of words in any passage we read in order to gain any understanding from it.

Types of reading

Adults need a range of reading styles to suit the complexity of the text and the purpose of reading it.

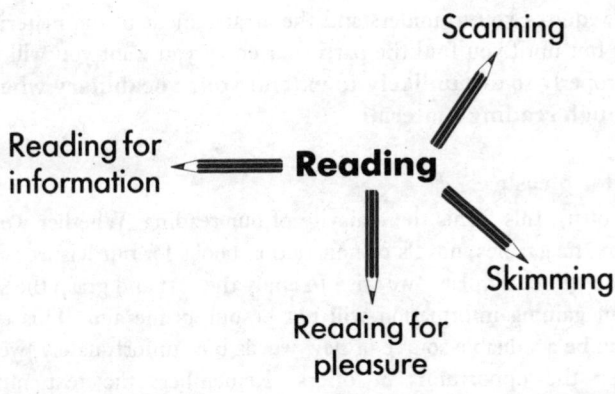

Skimming

A reader will skim through a text when he wishes to gain a general impression of the material.

You may do this when you are deciding which book to borrow from a library. You will have a brief look at the contents page and then glance at various passages in order to assess the subject matter, the writer's style, etc. You may also skim through a newspaper, reading a few headlines and noting articles of interest so you can return to read them properly later.

Skimming is a useful skill which enables you to 'get the gist' of a text but, as you will not be concentrating on understanding the text, **it is unlikely that you will develop your vocabulary by this type of reading.**

Scanning

Scanning allows you to search for a particular item in a text.

For example, if you wished to find the meaning of a word in a dictionary, you would:

  scan the guide words to locate the correct page, then
  scan the columns until you reach the required word.

Other examples of scanning include:

using timetables,

searching for phone numbers, and

finding a specific advertisement in the classified columns of a newspaper.

Scanning requires you to understand the arrangement of the material you are using, but until you find the particular entry you want you will not be reading properly so **are unlikely to extend your vocabulary when you scan through reading material.**

Reading for pleasure

For most of us, this forms the majority of our reading. Whether we select newspapers, magazines, novels or non-fiction books for our leisure reading, the purpose will be similar – we wish to enjoy the text and grasp the subject matter, but gaining information will not be our prime aim. This type of reading can be a valuable source of new words but, unfortunately, we don't always use the opportunity it offers. Remember, the text must be sufficiently demanding if we are to be exposed to unfamiliar words.

It would probably spoil your enjoyment if each time you came across a new word you rushed to a dictionary. As the new word will have been presented to you in a sentence you will often be able to guess its meaning, but do not leave it there. You should underline it or note it down so you can research it later. **By adopting a methodical approach towards new words, you will continue to enjoy reading and develop your vocabulary.**

The extract below and overleaf is the start of a Graham Greene story, *A Burnt-Out Case*. Read through the passage, adopting the advice given above for any words which you are uncertain of.

> The cabin-passenger wrote in his diary a parody of Descartes: 'I feel discomfort, therefore I am alive,' then sat pen in hand with no more to record. The captain in a white soutane stood by the open windows of the saloon reading his breviary. There was not enough air to stir the fringes of his beard. The two of them had been alone together on the river for ten days – alone, that is to say, except for the six members of the African crew and the dozen or so deck-passengers who changed, almost indistinguishably, at each village where they stopped. The boat, which was the property of the Bishop, resembled a small battered Mississippi paddle-steamer with a high nineteenth-century fore-structure, the white paint badly in need of renewal.

From the saloon windows they could see the river before them unwind, and below them on the pontoons the passengers sat and dressed their hair among the logs of wood for the engine.

If no change means peace, this certainly was peace, to be found like a nut at the centre of the hard shell of discomfort – the heat that engulfed them where the river narrowed to a mere hundred metres: the shower that was always hot from the ship's engine: in the evening the mosquitoes, and in the day the tsetse flies with wings raked back like tiny jet-fighters (a board above the bank at the last village had warned them in three languages: 'Zone of sleeping sickness. Be careful of the tsetse flies.'). The captain read his breviary with a fly-whisk in his hand, and whenever he made a kill he held up the tiny corpse for the passenger's inspection, saying 'tsetse' – it was nearly the limit of their communication, for neither spoke the other's language with ease or accuracy.

Reading for information or study purposes

In this type of reading vocabulary is very important as:

▶ in order to read effectively and be able to recall the salient facts, you will need to have a **complete understanding** of the words used

▶ you will probably encounter **demanding passages** containing unfamiliar or technical words

▶ by researching these new words you will **extend your vocabulary** in the subject

You may have to do such reading in the course of:

   your job (technical reports, instruction manuals, etc.)

   your everyday life (tax returns, benefit information, etc.)

   or your education or training (text books, revision notes, etc.)

Whatever the situation, it is essential that you understand the information you read. You will need to adopt an active approach to reading and make a positive effort to understand the text.

Your reading will become more effective if you follow these steps.

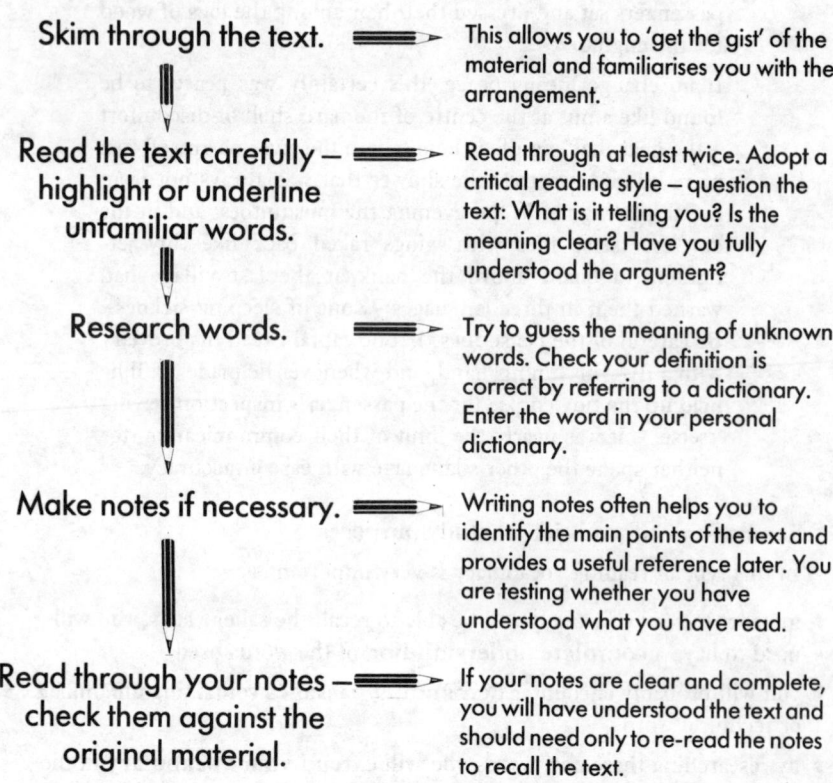

Skim through the text. ➤ This allows you to 'get the gist' of the material and familiarises you with the arrangement.

Read the text carefully – highlight or underline unfamiliar words. ➤ Read through at least twice. Adopt a critical reading style – question the text: What is it telling you? Is the meaning clear? Have you fully understood the argument?

Research words. ➤ Try to guess the meaning of unknown words. Check your definition is correct by referring to a dictionary. Enter the word in your personal dictionary.

Make notes if necessary. ➤ Writing notes often helps you to identify the main points of the text and provides a useful reference later. You are testing whether you have understood what you have read.

Read through your notes – check them against the original material. ➤ If your notes are clear and complete, you will have understood the text and should need only to re-read the notes to recall the text.

You might like to test your reading-for-information skills by reading the following passage on the history of spectacles. Follow the advice already given to you, making notes on the subject. You will have been successful if you are able to pass on the information accurately, using your notes as a prompt.

Spectacles

Transparent objects were used to help defective eyesight in antiquity: the best-known case is that of the Emperor Nero, who watched performances in the arena holding in front of one eye a jewel with curved facets; perhaps concave facets to correct shortsightedness. But such reports are rare and without scientific foundation.

Lenses placed close to the eyes were first certainly used towards the end of the 13th century. Nothing is known of the inventor, or of the date or place of the discovery, as it was the work of an illiterate artisan, but Edward Rosen fixes the period of the discovery to the five years after 1280. The inventor was probably a glazier, who made ornaments and glass discs for windows.

Lenses were given their name because of their resemblance in shape to lentils (the Italian for lens is *lente*, for lentils *lenticchie*) and for more than three centuries they were called glass lentils.

All lenses at this time were of the converging type. Despite the scientists' condemnation, artisans continued to make them as a remedy for long sight. They found that the older people became, the more accentuated the curve of their lenses needed to be.

While there are no exact records of the change brought about by the invention of spectacles, it must have played its part in revolutionizing man's attitude to the world. In its simplest aspect, it extended the working life of scholars and copyists; and in a more complex way it helped to demonstrate that man could be partially independent both of his physical limitations and of natural periods such as the length of daylight.

V.R.
(from *Eureka!*)

Difficulties with reading

Even if you are an excellent reader, you will probably find some reading material difficult to understand. Why?

Too much of the vocabulary may be unfamiliar.

You might be unfamiliar with the subject matter.

The style of writing could be elaborate, contorted or new to you.

Perhaps the sentences are too long and complicated.

Although style, sentence length and structure can present difficulties, it is unfamiliarity with vocabulary which really impedes understanding.

Read this passage.

C&T Develops Multiprocessing Design; Alternative to C-Bus

Attempting to provide an alternative to Corollary's C-Bus Intel-based multiprocessing architecture, Chips & Technologies (San Jose, CA) has developed its own multiprocessing platform called M/PAX.

M/PAX and its Corollary counterpart both support multiple processors in a single chassis, communicating with each other over a proprietary bus. But M/PAX's main advantage is the bandwidth of its interprocessor data channel, or Multi-Processor Interface; the MPI is a 128-bit-wide bus that passes messages between processors. M/PAX calls for an additional level of cache, beyond the i486 internal cache, to reduce the total traffic between the processors and to the shared memory pool. Up to four memory controllers can be present in an M/PAX implementation, permitting multiple simultaneous transfers.

Chips & Technologies provides the interface circuits needed for the system, processor, and memory modules. A company representative claimed that M/PAX has a significant performance edge over Corollary's C-Bus and said that the SCO MPX extensions to Unix work with both C-Bus and M/PAX. The same representative said that one drawback is that M/PAX may not support as many total processors as C-Bus.

—Tom Yager

(from *Byte* magazine)

Unless you are familiar with computer language, you probably found that:

> your reading was slow
>
> you had to re-read phrases or sentences to make sense of some of the words
>
> you can recall very little of what you read

Understanding the precise meaning of a word or group of words is a complex skill, but without it much of our reading becomes pointless and we fail to function effectively at college, work or home.

The next chapter will help you to develop strategies for understanding demanding material.

6
Reading and Understanding

Chapters 5 and 6 are concerned with the link between wide reading and an improved vocabulary. In Chapter 5 we looked at the reading process and the acquisition of vocabulary. In this chapter we will consider how we can gain a greater understanding from what we read and improve the quality of our reading.

Improving understanding

At school you will probably have been tested on your understanding of passages that you were asked to read. This will have happened in most subjects but in English it will have been formalised into a task called 'comprehension'.

The word 'comprehension' may, even now, conjure up a picture of your struggle with difficult and boring passages, full of unfamiliar words. Answering the questions was a painful task. But comprehension is not confined to school. It is a skill which you can actively develop so allowing you to:

> understand a greater variety of texts

> understand difficult texts more accurately

Everyday reading – advice

▶ Try to become a more active reader. Adopt a more critical, questioning style of reading.

▶ When you have finished reading, take time to assess the content and reflect on what you have gained from the text.

▶ You may like to pause in your reading and try to predict how the author will continue. Think about the words he might use, as well as how he will develop the theme.

By allowing yourself time and making a sustained effort, you will notice your comprehension skills will start to improve.

Coping with difficult passages

It will be helpful to refer to page 55, as the advice given there on developing a meticulous approach to reading will also help you to tackle difficult passages.

Here are some other strategies you might find useful.

▶ Read more slowly. Allow yourself time to absorb the information by concentrating on a small group of words at a time. Look carefully at particularly difficult phrases and sentences and consider what is meant.

▶ After you have read the passage, try to recall as many points as possible. Even if you are unable to write these down, compile a list in your mind.

▶ Imagine you are telling someone else about what you've read. Try putting it in your own words. If you are able to explain or recount the information, you will have understood it. If you have difficulties with any particular section, go back to the text and re-read that section.

Tackling unfamiliar words

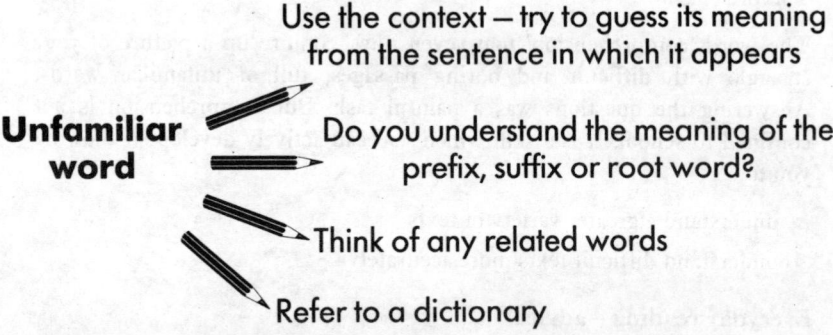

Unfamiliar word

Use the context – try to guess its meaning from the sentence in which it appears

Do you understand the meaning of the prefix, suffix or root word?

Think of any related words

Refer to a dictionary

Context

If you encounter an unfamiliar word within a sentence, it is possible to make a reasonable guess about the meaning of it provided you understand the rest of the sentence and are familiar with the subject matter. You may find it easier to decide on the meaning, and that your guess is more accurate if you can identify which part of speech the word is (verb, noun, adjective, etc.).

e.g. His **arbitrary** decision created confusion and argument.

Because of this word's relationship to the noun 'decision', we can assume that it is an adjective and describes the decision.

In the writer's opinion the decision 'created confusion and argument' so we could assume that it was a 'poor' decision.

We can consider why the decision might be 'poor': it could be

high–handed

ineffectual

made without reference to the situation

hasty

ill–considered

In fact, many of these guesses are close to the dictionary definition of arbitrary.

> **arbitrary**, of controlled power; despotic; deciding or decided
> on inadequate grounds

6

** Define the underlined words in the following sentences by considering the contexts in which they occur.

1 The calumny was repeated in the papers causing Mr Smith considerable distress.

2 Her capricious behaviour stopped others from relying upon her.

3 Peter tried to emulate his brother's athletic achievements.

4 In his summing up, the judge referred to the accused as having committed a heinous crime.

5 During a brief hiatus in the shooting, the soldiers were able to regroup.

Understanding prefixes and suffixes

Many words can be broken down into root word, prefix and/or suffix.

A root word is a base word before a prefix and/or suffix is added.

A prefix is a group of letters added to the beginning of a word. A prefix affects or alters the meaning of the root word.

A suffix is a group of letters added to the end of a root word which makes the word the correct part of speech for the sentence.

e.g. unhappiness

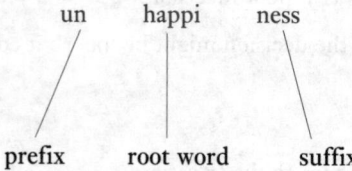

un   happi   ness

prefix   root word   suffix

(The addition of the suffix alters the 'y' of 'happy' to 'i')

It is often helpful to break up words in this way in order to establish their meanings. Understanding the meanings of prefixes is especially useful when tackling unfamiliar words as prefixes can provide vital clues.

EXAMPLES:

prefix	meaning
trans	across or through
transatlantic	across the Atlantic
transect	cut across
transfer	send or move to another place
transparent	allows light to pass through

prefix	meaning
mono	single
monogamy	being married to only one partner at a time
monomania	obsessed with a single idea
monopoly	exclusive possession of a trading right
monotonous	of one pitch, unvaried

** Using a dictionary, find the meaning of each prefix and then check that you know the meaning of each word listed under the prefix.

    hyper   syn   contra

    quad   mal   bene

Suffixes may not be quite as useful as prefixes in unlocking the meaning of words as many have no obvious meaning.

e.g. ate ——— fortunate

             proportionate

However, some suffixes do have quite clear meanings.

e.g.	suffix	meaning
	less	without
	thoughtless	without thought
	friendless	without friends
	careless	without care

Being aware of prefixes and suffixes can be a useful aid in tackling unfamiliar words. You may find it helpful to compile a list of prefixes and suffixes, together with their meanings.

Related words

Once you are aware of root words, prefixes and suffixes, you will notice how words belong to word families – and share similar meanings.

e.g.	grateful	thankful
	gratify	to please or indulge
	gratuity	gift in return for service
	gratuitous	performed without charge, freely given

All the words above belong to a word family based on the idea of giving pleasure or wishing to express pleasure.

By understanding the meaning of one or two words in a family, you can often make a reasonable attempt at working out the other words.

** Find the relationship between the words in each group. You may need to use a dictionary to check that you have the correct connection.

1 deficit	2 equilibrium	3 effective
deficient	equidistant	efficacious
	equitable	efficient
4 impetus	5 antipathy	6 cognition
impetuous	apathy	recognise
	sympathy	
	empathy	

Throughout this book we have recommended that you should try to define an unfamiliar word yourself before referring to a dictionary. This ensures that you think carefully about the word instead of just relying upon the dictionary to provide the answer. If you follow this procedure you will find that you are more confident about your own ability and more alive to words and their meanings.

Remember, always check that your definition is correct by comparing it with the dictionary's definition.

Formal comprehension

Comprehension in English examinations may take the form of:

▶ Cloze procedure
▶ Multiple choice
▶ Standard comprehension questions

Cloze procedure

This is a modern method of assessing comprehension skills. The process was described by its originator, Wilson Taylor, as 'completing the sentence pattern'. It is based on the theory that a fluent reader doesn't read every word in a passage but automatically fills in the gaps with his own words; the reader predicts what the writer has written by using context clues and his experience of language patterns.

I crawled into my bunk *by* 3 a.m.	I crawled into my bunk *at* 3 a.m.
and it seemed that I *had*	and it seemed that I *had*
hardly fallen asleep before I was	hardly fallen asleep before I was
awakened *by* the ship leaping	awakened *by* the ship leaping
and *lunching* like a wild thing.	and *bucking* like a wild thing.
completed cloze version	*writer's version*

In a cloze passage words are deleted from the text on a regular basis – generally every fifth to seventh word. If they were omitted more often than this, the reader would have difficulty making sense of the text. The reader has to supply an appropriate word which makes sense in the context of the passage: it may not be the word chosen by the writer. Only one word can be used to fill each gap.

Helpful Hints

▶ Read through the complete passage to understand the overall content.

▶ Read each sentence in turn, filling in the missing words.

▶ If you are unable to find a suitable word, continue with the rest of the passage. Return to the part you have difficulty with later – the addition of other words may help you.

▶ When you have completed the whole passage, re-read it, check that it makes sense and that the words you have supplied are the correct parts of speech.

** Now try to complete this cloze passage.

Without doubt the long hot summer of 1990 took its toll in terms of increases in the number of reported thefts and burglaries.

Figures for the second quarter .... 1990 showed a 17% rise .... recorded crime with marked .... in burglary and car crime.

These .... paint a gloomy picture, but .... is even more depressing is .... many of these crimes are opportunistic .... would not have happened if .... had been more aware. For .... , a third of domestic burglaries did .... involve forced entry as the householder .... left a door or window ....

Basic crime prevention costs little; in .... cases it costs nothing except .... time. There are various measures you can take to stop yourself being the victim of the opportunist.

Multiple choice comprehension

In this type of comprehension, candidates are questioned on a text and are provided with about four alternative answers. They have to select the answer that appears to be correct.

Answers are often marked on a special answer sheet which can be 'read' by a computer.

Helpful Hints

▶ Read the text carefully.

▶ Study each question – decide exactly what is being asked.

▶ Read the alternative answers carefully.

▶ Look back to the text and test each answer against the relevant part of the text. The examiner may try to confuse you with a word that appears similar or by a statement that is almost correct.

▶ When you have made your choice of answer, make sure you enter it correctly on the answer sheet.

▶ You will need to be accurate both in your reading and your recording.

▶ Always answer all the questions.

▶ If you are uncertain, make a guess. Similarly, if you run out of time, mark off the answers at random – you may be lucky and pick a right answer!

** Practise this technique in the passage below.

Douglas Fir Pseudotsuga Douglasii Introduced into Britain in 1872.

Douglas Fir is very variable in type, but it makes a fine specimen when grown in suitable positions. The timber is valuable and it has been used chiefly as a forest tree in this country but it is beautiful when grown in the open.

Under forest conditions its outstanding feature is its great height and straight trunk, free of branches and tapering very gradually.

Planting Small plants under one metre high transplant best in early autumn or late spring.

Growth Fast growing often exceeding 60cm a year for the first 20 or 30 years. Very tall and graceful, Douglas Fir is a long lived tree and may reach a height of over 100 metres and a diameter of 5.5 metres when it is hundreds of years old.

The main stem persists to the tip of the tree and the lateral branches are comparatively slender and slightly drooping.

Soil Moist soils of many types. Only in very moist atmospheric conditions can Douglas Fir endure dry sandy soils. It will grow on moist acid soil and even on the edge of brackish water.

Climate In Britain, Douglas Fir is extremely hardy against frost, but dislikes very windy positions. It enjoys the moist atmosphere of our western and northern zones.

Habitat This tree is found on the Pacific coast from British Columbia to Mexico and inland as far as the east side of the Rockies, in some parts up to an altitude of 6,000 feet. Forests of pure Douglas Fir are found and it also occurs in mixed woods.

Fig. 0119

1 Refer to Fig. 0119.
  Small plants under one metre high transplant best in
  a mid summer or late autumn
  b early winter or early spring
  c late summer or late autumn
  d early autumn or late spring.

2 According to Fig. 0119, the best conditions for the growth of the
  Douglas Fir are
  a moist soil and atmosphere and sheltered position
  b dry atmosphere, sheltered position on the edge of brackish water
  c dry atmosphere, windy position, in dry sandy soil
  d moist soil and atmosphere, in windy position.

3 Fig. 0119 states that Douglas Fir trees
  a are found as far as the east side of the Rockies
  b are not found in Britain
  c are usually found above 6,500 feet
  d never occur in mixed woods.

4 The most important characteristic of the Douglas Fir to a forester
  growing the tree commercially for timber is its
  a beautiful appearance when grown in the open
  b ability to grow in moist soil
  c long straight-grain timbers of substantial cross-section
  d ability to grow at an altitude of 6,000 feet.

Standard comprehension questions

In comprehension tests candidates are required to read the text and then provide their own answers to a variety of questions. It is important to understand the type of question being asked and appreciate what is expected in the answer. The number of marks awarded to each question will help you to determine the amount of detail required in each answer.

Examining the questions

Read through the text in the example paper several times and then read the questions carefully, noting the different ways the questions 'test' comprehension.

     "A name," said Jeannie. "We must have a signboard outside the house giving the name of the inn. They all do."

     "I suppose we could call it 'The Red Lion' or 'The White Hart'," said Gladys flippantly, "though I think my mother would be a bit shocked if she thought I'd come all the way to China to work as a barmaid in 'The Red Lion'."   5

     Jeannie Lawson laughed. "I've got it," she said. "A wonderful name . . . 'The Inn of Eight Happinesses'. Isn't that good?"

A few days later the inn was officially open. The smell of good food eddied out from Yang's kitchen, and they waited patiently for the first customers! Muleteers crowded into the inn opposite, and the ones farther down the street. Muleteers and carriers plodded past, looking up at the inviting sign of 'The Inn of Eight Happinesses', but no one came into the hostelry of the 'foreign devils'. Obviously they were being boycotted. 10

15

Jeannie held a council of war. They decided that more seductive, or forceful, measures would have to be taken.

"You," said Jeannie, levelling a stubby finger at Gladys, "will be responsible for bringing the customers into the courtyard." 20

"But how?" protested Gladys.

Jeannie chattered questioningly in Chinese to Yang. He nodded his bald head in agreement.

Apparently, according to him, there was a physical psychology attached to bringing a customer into a Yangcheng hostelry that was unique in the accommodation business. Some of the staider muleteers made reservations at the same inn every time they passed through. You did not try to poach them—that was unethical; but there were many other casual visitors. When a muleteer came down the track looking to left and right at the inn signs, you took it that he was a casual. Legitimate prey! Then the innkeeper who stood bland and benign at his courtyard door went into action. As the lead mule passed he made a grab at the animal's head and tried to drag it in the direction of his own courtyard. The other mules were all tethered behind him with no choice but to follow. That, said Jeannie Lawson, was going to be Gladys's job. 25

30

35

ALAN BURGESS

(a) Choose **four** of the following words. For each word chosen give another word or short phrase which could replace it in the passage without change of meaning.

plodded (line 14)   agreement (line 23)

responsible (line 20)   poach (line 28)

chattered (line 22)   unethical (line 29) (*4 marks*)

(b) Explain *in your own* words the meaning of each of the following expressions as it is used in the passage:

(i) held a council of war (line 17);

(ii) took it that he was a casual (line 31).   (*4 marks*)

(c) What reason does Jeannie give for the need to have a signboard outside their inn?   (*2 marks*)

(d) For what **two** reasons might customers have been attracted to their inn? *(2 marks)*

(e) Explain in your own words why the keepers of 'The Inn of Eight Happinesses' were boycotted. *(2 marks)*

(f) From the passage, quote the part of a sentence which suggests that Jeannie and Gladys considered very different steps to obtain customers. *(2 marks)*

(g) *In your own words*, describe how an innkeeper gained a 'casual' customer (lines 33 – 37). *(4 marks)*

When you have read this, look at the advice below about responding to this particular paper.

Helpful Hints

Question **(a)** requires you to understand each word as it is used in the passage and provide an alternative word or phrase. Test your alternative word or phrase by substituting it into the relevant sentence – check it has the correct meaning for that context and it is the correct part of speech.

Question **(b)** assesses your understanding of the two phrases by asking you to explain their meanings. Before writing your explanations, refer to the appropriate parts of the text – your explanations must be relevant to the passage.

Questions **(c)** and **(d)** have their answers in the text – close reading will locate them but remember you haven't been asked to quote from the text so give the answers briefly in your own words.

Question **(e)** requires you to find the reason and demonstrate that you understand the word 'boycotted'. The text implies that the keepers of the inn were boycotted because they were considered to be 'foreign devils'; this phrase also needs to be explained in your answer.

Question **(f)** requires you to quote from the passage. The answer is not obvious and demands some careful reading to locate. Remember to quote the actual words from the passage. You are asked to quote only *part of the sentence.*

Question **(g)** not only assesses your understanding of the final few lines which contain words like 'bland', 'benign' and 'tethered', but also asks you to combine ideas from three sentences. Notice that four marks are awarded for this answer so you need to provide a sufficient number of points in your answer.

From this study of a typical comprehension paper you will appreciate the necessity of having a full and varied vocabulary in order to answer the questions. Your success may also depend on your technique.

▶ Read through the passage carefully several times.

▶ Identify any difficult words and try to guess their meanings. If possible, check your ideas in a dictionary.

▶ Try to identify the main points and express them in your own words.

▶ Briefly read through all the questions before starting to answer any of them. This will stop your answers from overlapping. You may also find it helpful to mark the text where you think each answer may be found.

▶ Number your answers correctly.

▶ If you have difficulty answering a question, try rephrasing the question in your own words.

▶ Answer in sentences, using your own words unless you are instructed differently.

▶ Check your answers.

Even if you are not involved in English examinations, looking at exam papers and books containing examples of comprehension questions extends and develops your vocabulary; the passages have been deliberately chosen by examiners to stretch the candidates' abilities.

The reading circle

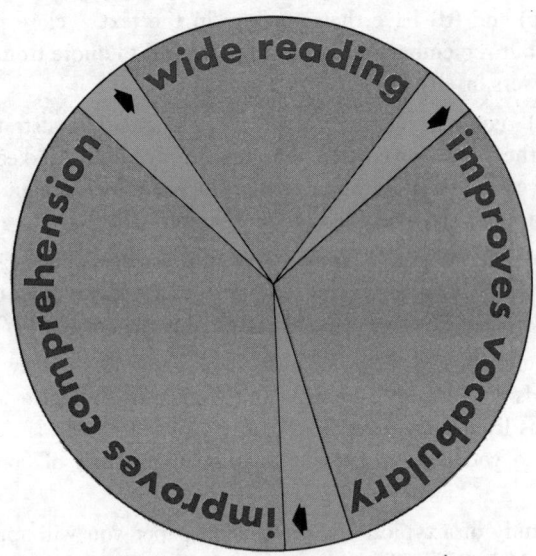

Chapters 5 and 6 have looked in some depth at the relationship between reading and vocabulary. We hope they illustrate the importance of a wide vocabulary and how it can increase your understanding and enjoyment of what you read. This can be summed up as <u>the reading circle</u>.

6

7
Get It Right

Making mistakes

It is inevitable that we will make mistakes as we acquire new words because:

we have failed to listen carefully so we confuse similar sounding words, or

we have not quite understood the meaning of a word or the way it is used so we misapply it.

Don't worry too much about making mistakes when you first try out new words. It is only with practice that they will become part of your natural vocabulary.

Our speech and writing may also become inaccurate and rely too much on tired phrases because:

we have become careless, or

we lack sufficient rigorous practice, or

we have few opportunities to develop a formal, precise writing style.

Whatever the reasons for mistakes, it is important that we know what is acceptable and are able to identify and correct our own errors.

You may have seen or read Sheridan's play *The Rivals* in which Dolly Malaprop (from whom the word 'malapropism' originated) makes us laugh with such lines as:

> " But the point we would request of you
> Is, that you will promise to forget this fellow —
> to illiterate him, I say, quite from your memory."

It is often easy to spot other people's errors but remain unaware of our own. This chapter provides an introduction to some areas of vocabulary which can create difficulties and detract from the strength and accuracy of writing.

- Common confusions
- 'Precise' words
- Colloquial language
- Clichés
- Tautology
- Verbosity
- Jargon

Before you study this chapter, it may be helpful to skim through it to see which parts are of particular interest and relevance to you. Sections 2 and 3 give more extensive help and practice in some of these areas.

Common confusions

Should we say

The drunken driver <u>flaunted</u> the law.

or

The drunken driver <u>flouted</u> the law?

> **flaunt**, display ostentatiously or offensively; wave proudly
>
> **flout**, show scorn of; treat with contempt

By comparing dictionary definitions of the words, we see that the second sentence is correct.

It is easy to confuse such pairs of words as they sound similar. We may even start to emulate Mrs Malaprop!

Helpful Hints

- Become a more attentive listener – often such confusions occur because we fail to discriminate between similar sounding words.
- Always check the meanings of unfamiliar words in a dictionary.
- Adopt a careful approach when proof-reading your writing. Be critical of what you have written and try to read it as if it were written by someone else – this should make you more effective at identifying your mistakes.
- Collect examples of confusing pairs of words. If you include these in your personal dictionary, highlight or underline the visual differences between the two words and show the meaning of each word together with an example of the way each is used.

EXAMPLE:

judicious	judicial
having sound judgement	connected with a court
showing wisdom and	of law
good sense	
e.g. Having considered the	e.g. The judicial hearing was
options carefully, he	set for November 9th at
made a judicious decision	Winchester Crown Court.
and accepted the job they	
had offered him.	

** The following pairs of words are frequently confused. Try to differentiate between each word in the pair. If you are uncertain of the meanings, check them in your dictionary and record the words in your personal dictionary.

alternate	alternative
disinterested	uninterested
official	officious
momentary	momentous
abuse	misuse
adverse	averse
ambiguous	ambivalent
censor	censure
comprehend	apprehend
credible	creditable
illusion	allusion
illegible	ineligible
oral	aural

'Precise' words

Look at these two sentences.

1 The second vote was more unanimous than the first. ✗

2 Their house is very unique. ✗

Neither sentence is correct.

Sentence 1 'Unanimous' means 'all of one opinion; with no dissent'. A vote is unanimous if everyone agrees, so one vote cannot be more unanimous than another.

Sentence 2 A house is 'unique' if it is the only one of its kind. It cannot be *more* than 'unique'.

In these sentences the words 'more' and 'very' are unnecessary. **Absolutes such as 'unique' and 'unanimous' cannot be qualified or compared.**

Here are some other examples of misuse.

It was <u>totally</u> <u>necessary</u> to leave that night. (Omit 'totally' as 'necessary' is sufficient on its own.)

It was <u>nearly</u> <u>essential</u> to pass the examination. (Either omit 'nearly' if it *was* essential, or replace 'nearly essential' with 'important'.)

She was <u>very</u> <u>immaculately</u> dressed. (Omit 'very'.)

The house was <u>extremely</u> <u>silent</u>. (Omit 'extremely'.)

Such mistakes occur in our speech when we are trying to create effect and stimulate our listener's interest.

Although technically incorrect, in informal situations such mistakes are acceptable. However, in formal interviews or writing tasks we should always avoid such inaccuracy.

Helpful Hints

▶ Before selecting a word to qualify or intensify another word, consider:

Do you need that extra word?

Are you trying to heighten or lessen the effect of what is already an absolute?

▶ Be selective in your choice of words – by overusing words like extremely, very, totally, completely or absolutely you can lessen the impact of your writing.

Colloquial language

> **colloquial** [ko/*Ok*wi-al] *adj* used in informal
> speech, characteristic of everyday conversation ~
> **colloquially** *adv* ~ **colloquialism** *n* colloquial word
> or expression.
> (from *Penguin English Dictionary*)

In informal situations colloquial language is perfectly acceptable; we know the person we are talking to and use the language appropriate to that relationship.

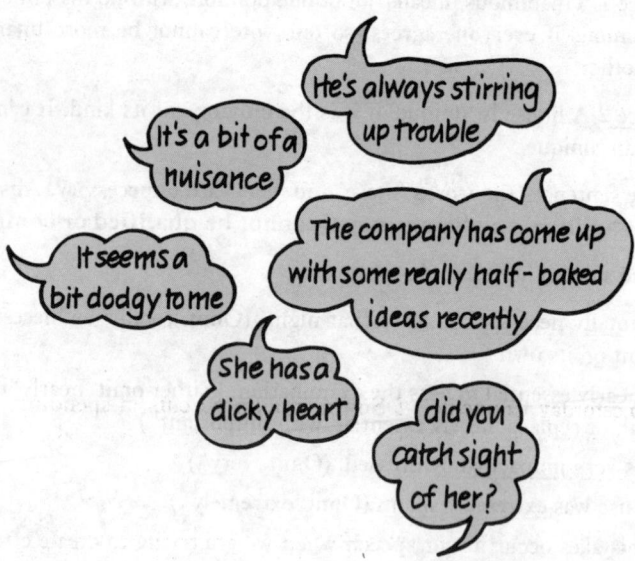

In formal situations, whether speaking or writing, we should avoid colloquial language.

Why?

Although colourful, colloquialisms can be imprecise. For example how would you 'half bake' an idea?

Language should always be appropriate for the situation and audience. In formal situations, formal language is required. Failure to use the appropriate vocabulary can cause embarrassment.

Using colloquial expressions stops us from developing our vocabulary. Such language is an indication of a careless, easily satisfied approach towards vocabulary. It is worth spending time selecting a more exact and considered word or phrase.

** Rewrite each of the colloquial sentences above, replacing the colloquial word or phrase with more formal language.

Avoiding colloquial language

Most dictionaries identify which words or phrases are colloquial. If you are uncertain as to the suitability of a word or phrase, check it in a dictionary.

Refer to Chapter 8 for suitable alternatives to some common colloquial words.

Become more aware of colloquial language. Listen to conversations more carefully. Try to decide whether the language used has the appropriate level of formality.

Practise using more formal language. (Chapters 12 and 13 provide you with some formal writing tasks.)

Clichés

cliché (kleeshay) n. stereotyped, hackneyed expression

See if you can identify the clichés in this newspaper report.

> ### COUNCIL ANNOUNCES SPENDING BREAKTHROUGH
>
> Yesterday Councillor E Smith announced cuts in spending amounting to a staggering £200,000. "These savings have been made," Councillor Smith declared, "by swingeing cuts in costs. No stone has been left unturned. Every avenue explored. In this day and age, our residents have a right to expect the Council to come up with a blueprint for success to ensure high standards of service at a rock bottom price."

Often local and national newspapers seem to include as many clichés as possible in a story. Although it is unlikely that a story will contain as many clichés as the example above, we are all too frequently told of 'breakthroughs', 'swingeing' cuts and 'blueprints for success', until the words lose their impact and become meaningless. Unfortunately, because we are so frequently exposed to such tired phrases, we may inadvertently include them in our speech and writing. Such expressions can be irritating to our audience and rarely contribute to the variety and content of our speech or writing.

Helpful Hints

▶ Listen carefully to your own speech. Try to express your ideas clearly – avoid clichés.

▶ Proof-read your writing.

▶ Clichés such as 'in actual fact' and 'at this moment in time' can be replaced by a simple word or phrase. Try using 'in fact' instead of 'in actual fact' and 'now' instead of 'at this moment in time'.

▶ You might find it interesting to browse through Eric Partridge's *Dictionary of Clichés* and *Dictionary of Catch Phrases*. You will notice that clichés have a brief spell of popularity before quickly becoming dated and forgotten – which is another reason for avoiding them.

** Rewrite the newspaper article on council spending, replacing tired, hackneyed phrases with more interesting language. You should find that your article is livelier and has more variety than the original.

Tautology

What is wrong with these sentences?

1 David descended down into the mine. ✗

2 Please return the newspaper back where it belongs. ✗

3 This wonderful new innovation will improve our lives. ✗

4 When you first begin to drive, there is a great deal to remember. ✗

5 The writers collaborated together. ✗

Each sentence contains an unnecessary repetitive word; it is tautologous.

> tautology [taw*tol*oji] *n* unnecessary repetition
> of the same idea in different words.
>
> (from *Penguin English Dictionary*)

<u>Sentence 1</u> 'descend down': descend means 'to go down' so 'down' can be omitted from the sentence.

<u>Sentence 2</u> 'return . . . back': return means 'put back' so omit 'back'.

<u>Sentence 3</u> 'new innovation': an innovation means 'new' so omit 'new'.

<u>Sentence 4</u> 'first begin': omit 'first' as 'begin' is sufficient.

<u>Sentence 5</u> 'collaborate together': omit 'together' as 'collaborate' means 'work together'.

When proof-reading your writing, carefully consider the precise meanings of words and whether each is fulfilling a useful function in the sentence. By understanding the exact definition of a word, you will be able to identify any unnecessary words and avoid tautology.

** Remove the unnecessary word from each of these sentences.

1 The two teams combined together to raise money for charity.

2 He repeated the word again.

3 It was necessary to separate the two dogs apart.

4 The doctor mentioned about the surgery's closure next week.

5 The electricity supply has been connected up.

Verbosity

This can be defined as using an excessive number of words or long, complicated words and phrases to express a simple idea.

EXAMPLES:

He replied in the affirmative.

She actioned the memo to facilitate a more advantageous situation.

Perhaps the writer of these two sentences is trying to impress the reader with his or her vocabulary; perhaps he or she imagines that long words and involved sentences are 'better' than direct simple sentences.

We don't wish to limit your choice of words or discourage you from using a variety of sentence constructions, but clarity and precision should always be your aim.

Try to choose the exact word; it may not always be the longest. Write in clear sentences: long, complex sentences can obscure meaning.

| Helpful Hints |

Most everyday writing tasks require a clear, direct style. Avoid expressing your ideas in unnecessarily abstract words or phrases.

e.g. The residence is situated in a favourable situation, receiving the benefit of the sun's position in relation to the building.

This could be rewritten:

The house faces south.

Consider your audience. **Choose words and sentence constructions that are appropriate both for the task and the reader.**

Verbose sentences suggest that the writer is uncertain of his or her own vocabulary and is hoping, by adopting such a style, to create the right impression. **Be confident about your English.** Practice is one of the most effective ways to improve and develop confidence. You may find home study a useful way to gain practice, or perhaps you would prefer to join a writing class at a local college.

A verbose style may be used when a writer is uncertain of the content of the writing. He may not have a clear idea of what he is trying to convey. Careful planning can eliminate this uncertainty and the vagueness that it creates.

Where appropriate, replace a phrase with a single word.

e.g. In view of his lack of punctuality his employment was terminated.

<u>As</u> he was <u>unpunctual</u>, he was <u>dismissed</u>.

When proof-reading your writing, check that you have expressed your ideas clearly and concisely. Remove any redundant words or phrases.

Jargon

> **Jargon**, the words and phrases used by a group of people in connection with their job or interest.

Colloquially, we would call it 'talking shop'. For members of the group, jargon can be useful as it often expresses a complex idea in a single, simple word or phrase.

EXAMPLES:

Do you know what a 'glitch' is?

Have you experienced 'chalk and talk'?

Have you ever met a 'twitcher'?

Although such language is understood by the group's members, it can be incomprehensible to others. Jargon is also subject to changes in fashion, particularly in areas such as computing and selling, so it quickly becomes outdated.

It is acceptable to use jargon within the group which understands it, but we should avoid using it in general communication.

Final thoughts

As we said at the start of this chapter, when you are learning new words you will probably make mistakes but don't let this stop you from extending your vocabulary. An awareness of common errors and careful proof-reading should eliminate most mistakes from your writing. **Remember, your aim is to communicate effectively, which includes selecting the appropriate language both for your audience and the situation.** Consideration of these points should help you to get it right.

** Read this extract from a letter about changes in benefits in which scant consideration has been given to the reader: little attempt has been made to express a difficult subject in simple language.

An extract from a council letter:

"Where a claimant's income is below his/ her applicable amount, he/she will qualify for benefit to cover 100 per cent of the eligible rent and 80 per cent of eligible rates.

"Where the claimant's income is higher than their applicable amount, there are only two tapers (ie the percentage of the difference between income and the applicable amount, which is deducted from the eligible rent and rates to determine entitlement)..."

To Sum Up

Section 1 has given you considerable guidance on developing your vocabulary, and advice on how to express yourself clearly and accurately. Sections 2 and 3 will give you the structured practice that is so important if you are actively to extend your vocabulary. Before you continue, you may like to assess your progress so far.

▶ Have your dictionary skills improved?

▶ Can you use a thesaurus effectively?

▶ Are you compiling a personal dictionary?

▶ Are you continuing to research new words and becoming more skilful at using them correctly?

▶ Are you discovering new words when you read?

If you are able to see progress in these directions, you have begun to assimilate the ideas introduced to you in Section 1.

8
Conversational Words

In this chapter you will be introduced to:

words which dictionaries define as being 'colloquial';

words which, although not defined as colloquial, are more suited to informal conversation than formal speech and writing.

For each key word a range of synonyms is provided so that you can avoid the colloquial or conversational word. There are a number of activities to work through which will help you to remember the alternative vocabulary.

Colloquial and conversational words

mad

tell off

fed up

upset

funny

great .

lots of

kind of or sort of

thing or things

hard or difficult

dear

give up

mad

How many times have you said, 'He makes me so mad!' or 'I'm mad with her.'?

You will also have read sentences such as those below.

I was mad with Sylvia when she borrowed my bike without permission.

Jack never offered to help with the washing up which made his mother mad.

In all these examples 'mad' is being used in its colloquial sense meaning 'angry'.

The true meaning of 'mad' is 'insane' or 'recklessly foolish'. Why use 'mad' when there are so many other words which mean angry?

irate	indignant
enraged	furious
outraged	fuming
affronted	displeased
vexed	peevish
exasperated	riled
incensed	annoyed
irritated	disturbed
infuriated	offended

Careful selection enables us to express ourselves exactly; we can precisely describe our degree of anger, from being 'annoyed' or 'irritated' to being 'furious' or 'fuming'.

** If any of these words is new to you, look up its precise meaning in a dictionary. Try to arrange the words above into groups according to the degree of anger they express.

'Anger' is a noun, referring to the state of being angry. The following nouns also express degrees of anger or displeasure.

wrath   ire   pique   spleen   animosity

** Check their exact meanings in a dictionary, then add other synonyms for 'anger' to this list.

Helpful Hints

▶ I am always cross on Monday mornings.

'Cross' is frequently used to show displeasure. It is a conversational word when used in this way so it is best to avoid it.

tell off

EXAMPLES:

Philippa was told off by Miss Hedges.

I will tell you off if you do that again.

He was frightened of being told off.

The child worried about the telling off he'd receive at home.

'tell off' means 'scold' or 'chide'. It is frequently used in conversation.

What other words could be used?

reprimand	admonish
chastise	rebuke
reprehend	berate
castigate	censure
correct	discipline
upbraid	lecture
nag	remonstrate with
reproach	reprove
revile	vituperate

All of these verbs have a slightly different meaning and paint a particular shade of meaning.

** Use your dictionary to help you answer these questions. Which word or words from the list could be used:

to blame yourself;

to 'tell off' someone in an abusive manner;

to 'tell off' mildly?

There are other conversational expressions which are used to express 'a telling off'.

tick off	dress down
go on at	bawl out
haul over the coals	tear off a strip

** Replace the underlined words in these sentences with more precise, formal words.

1 The new recruit was <u>hauled over the coals</u> by the colour sergeant.

2 As Lisa had forgotten to post his letter, he would <u>tear her off a strip</u> in the morning.

3 The timid student was embarrassed by the <u>dressing down</u> he received.

4 Nigel was accustomed to being <u>ticked off</u> for minor misdemeanours.

5 He hated being <u>bawled out</u> in front of his friends.

6 Alex was frequently accused of <u>going on at</u> his wife.

fed up

When we want to express displeasure with a situation or with life in general, we often say we are 'fed up', or use the expression 'fed up to the teeth' or 'fed up to the back teeth'. Although it gives a general impression of how we are feeling, it doesn't paint a particularly clear picture for our audience. Why have we had 'too much'?

Alternatives to 'fed up'

I'm fed up with work.

I find work <u>tiring</u> and <u>tedious</u>.

He is fed up with exams.

He is <u>exhausted</u> by the exams.

My aunt is fed up with the same routine.

My aunt is <u>weary</u> of the same routine.

Lilian was fed up because she hadn't heard from her boyfriend.

Lilian was <u>troubled</u> because she hadn't heard from her boyfriend.

In each of these pairs of sentences, the second sentence gives a more exact picture than the first. The suggested alternatives and the words in the panel below may help you to explain your feelings more exactly so that you can avoid using 'fed up'.

worn out by	nauseated by	annoyed by	vexed by

** Use the words in the panel to replace the underlined words in each sentence.

1 The elderly tourist was <u>fed up with</u> the sight of so many undernourished children.

2 Ursula was <u>fed up with</u> his interference and his unwelcome offers of help.

3 The receptionist was <u>fed up with</u> her supervisor's attitude.

4 The nurse was <u>fed up with</u> climbing the four flights of stairs to the pharmacy.

When asked why we are 'fed up' with something, we often reply by using the vague word 'boring'.

wearisome	unexciting
commonplace	monotonous
mundane	routine
tedious	tiresome

** Match each of these definitions to one of the words in the list opposite.

dull and commonplace	repetitious
causing annoyance	uninteresting
never changing	stale
happening over and over again	unvaried
not holding the attention	irksome
no longer fresh	humdrum

upset

How did Sam really feel?

annoyed?

were his feelings hurt?

offended?

distressed?

More exact words to replace 'upset'

disturbed	ruffled
unsettled	agitated
dismayed	disconcerted

flustered	shocked
worried	grieved
confused	overwrought
feeling of disquiet	perturbed

Each of these words would give a more accurate picture of how 'upset' Sam was.

** Use your dictionary to check the exact meaning of any words you are uncertain of, then arrange the words under the appropriate headings.

<u>slightly</u> upset   <u>extremely</u> upset

** Complete the sentences, showing how the upset has occurred.

1 Bill was overwrought ....

2 His agitated state ....

3 You could see the waitress was flustered ....

4 .... had perturbed her.

5 Marjorie was merely ruffled ....

6 Shushma had a feeling of disquiet as ....

** What is the opposite of feeling 'upset'?

You feel 'calm', 'tranquil' or 'unperturbed'. Use your thesaurus to find other words to describe such an untroubled state.

funny

All of these statements are vague in meaning. Is 'funny' being used in its proper sense meaning 'amusing', or in its colloquial sense meaning 'odd'?

'Funny' should never be used in its colloquial sense in formal situations.

Replacing 'funny', meaning 'amusing'

Some of the words in the circle are synonyms for 'funny', others are antonyms. Check any unfamiliar words in your dictionary and then separate the words into two lists headed antonyms and synonyms.

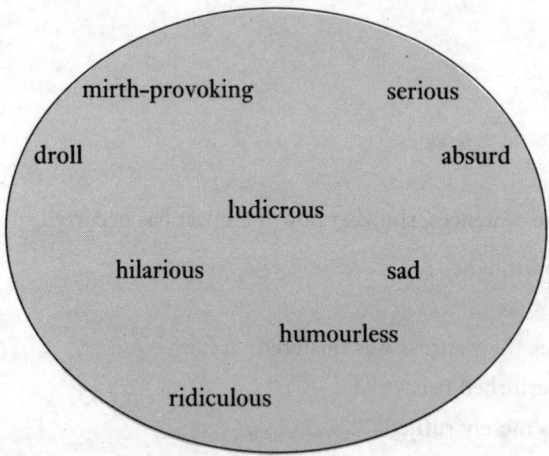

** Using a thesaurus, find additional synonyms and antonyms for 'funny' and add these to the appropriate list.

'funny' meaning 'odd' or 'unusual'

'Funny' used in this sense is a word used in informal conversation, but our conversation would be richer and more interesting if we avoided it. Its use is so common that it covers a wide range of meanings from 'slightly unusual' to 'extraordinary'.

Here are some typical everyday uses of 'funny'.

funny expression on his face	funny life style
a funny gadget	funny handle
wears funny clothes	a funny way of waggling his ears
a funny voice	a funny high colour to his cheeks
a funny plant	a funny design
funny behaviour	a funny statue

** Find a word or words from the panel below which can replace 'funny' in each of the above phrases.

unusual	eccentric	unnatural
exceptional	unconventional	alien
unorthodox	awkward	quaint
bizarre	singular	weird
Bohemian	unfamiliar	abnormal
freakish	extraordinary	outlandish
curious	strange	rare
peculiar	grotesque	remarkable
uncanny	unaccustomed	

Helpful Hints

▶ 'odd' could be used to replace 'funny' in all of these situations, but like 'funny' it occurs so frequently in our conversation that it fails to make an impact. It is only by using a range of words that we are able to give precision to our speech and writing.

great

The true meanings of 'great' are :

large,
important,
distinguished,
held in high esteem, or
highly gifted.

EXAMPLES:

The Mississippi is a great American waterway. (large and important)

He was a great statesman. (held in high esteem, distinguished and highly gifted)

London is one of the great financial capitals of the world. (important)

'Great' is used colloquially to mean 'excellent' or 'extremely enjoyable'. This use should be confined to informal speech but even then it would give your audience a fuller picture if you used more descriptive words.

EXAMPLES:

John's **great**. ✗   John is kind and helpful. ✓

We had a **great** game of football. ✗

We had a tiring but exhilarating game of football. ✓

What are the alternatives?

If you want to describe someone or something as being 'excellent', you could use one of the words below.

admirable	exquisite	meritorious
outstanding	exemplary	first-class
notable	prime	superb
superior	superlative	eminent
remarkable	noteworthy	perfect
	exceptional	

** Match these words to their definitions.

exquisite	deserving honour or reward
exemplary	of outstanding delicacy or beauty
meritorious	worthy of notice or imitation
eminent	superior to all others
superlative	distinguished, rising above others

** Use your thesaurus to find antonyms for 'excellent', beginning and ending with the following letters.

s _ _ _ _ _ _ _ _ d

im _ _ _ _ _ t

f _ _ _ y

in _ _ _ _ r

d _ _ _ _ d

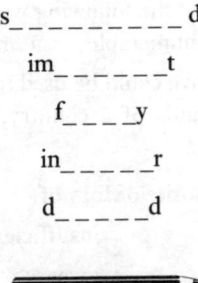

lots of

'Lots of' is acceptable in informal conversation.

EXAMPLES:

I have lots of money.

My father has lots of fillings.

Other words to use

abounding	abundant/abundance
countless	bounteous/bountiful
numerous	copious
numberless	infinite
innumerable	profuse
endless	overflowing
unnumbered	multitudinous
myriad	teeming

Some of these words can be used in sentences to directly replace 'lots of'; others can only be used if you restructure your sentences.

EXAMPLES:

There were lots of flowers in the small garden.

There were numerous flowers in the small garden.

There was a profusion of flowers in the small garden.

There was an infinite variety of flowers in the small garden.

**1 Use your dictionary to find the number that was originally associated with 'myriad'.

2 What is the shared meaning of the following words?

unnumbered   endless   innumerable   numberless   countless

3 Which word from the list above could be used to describe a harvest that was sufficient to meet the demands of a country, but not vastly beyond its needs?

These words express the opposite of **lots of**.

inadequate	deficient	insufficient	sparse
few	paltry	meagre	scarcity

** Using your dictionary to check meanings and a thesaurus to find related words, add to this list words which can be used to express the idea of there being 'little' of anything.

---

kind of and sort of

EXAMPLES:

Trudy had a kind of wild appearance.

Gavin said he had a sort of pain in his left shoulder.

Such expressions are unnecessary and should be avoided as they do not add detail to speech or writing but introduce an air of uncertainty. They could more accurately be written:

Trudy had a wild appearance.

Gavin said he had a pain in his left shoulder.

If you want to be more descriptive, precise words can be added.

Trudy had a wild, unkempt appearance.

Gavin said he had an acute pain in his left shoulder.

If, on the other hand, you really intend to be less definite, then express this in other ways.

At times Trudy had a wild, unkempt appearance.

When Trudy was at home, she took little trouble with her appearance and looked wild and unkempt.

Gavin said that he had an occasional slight pain in his left shoulder.

At times Gavin had an acute twinge of pain in his left shoulder.

** Rewrite these sentences, avoiding the underlined phrases.

> e.g. The dog was a <u>kind of</u> labrador.
>
> The dog was a crossbred labrador – part labrador, part collie.

1 Mike <u>sort of</u> expected Clara to refuse.

2 I dislike his <u>kind of</u> aggressive manner.

3 My friends have <u>sort of</u> ignored me since I went to work in Exeter.

4 Mrs Owen imposed a <u>kind of</u> discipline on her two sons.

5 Lizzy was <u>sort of</u> confused when Graham invited her to stay for the weekend.

---

thing or things

EXAMPLES:

I left my things in the car.

Karen has things to complete.

Anthony has a thing about spiders.

We can only understand the first two sentences if we can see the 'things' or know what is being referred to.

In the third statement 'thing' is being used in a colloquial way to replace 'obsession', 'phobia' or 'fixation'.

'Thing' or 'things' can only give our audience a vague impression of what we really want to say. It doesn't take much more effort to use the exact word or words.

> I left my shopping bag and briefcase in the car.
>
> Karen has letters to complete.

Is there a definite 'thing'?

EXAMPLE:

He doesn't explain things clearly.

People say he is guilty of wicked things

What's the name of that thing?

In informal conversation we frequently use such sentences, but 'thing' or 'things' gives a very unclear picture and in formal speech and writing we need to be more precise.

> He doesn't explain concepts clearly.
>
> People say he is guilty of wicked deeds.
>
> What's the name of that piece of apparatus?

Using other words

According to the situation, it is possible to add more variety to your conversation and writing by using words such as those listed below.

apparatus	*gadget	tool
deed	aspect	event
article	instrument	*feat
equipment	*contrivance	object
*phenomenon	possessions	device
affair	*implement	*impedimenta
instrument	circumstances	*facet
*substance	fact	item
mechanism	matter	feature

** Use your dictionary to check the exact meanings of the words with asterisks. From memory, write a brief definition for each word.

hard and difficult

> Advanced maths was too hard for me

> There are so many hard steps to learn

TUESDAY   **FEBRUARY**

I had a difficult day at work. I had to complete several difficult reports, deal with a difficult customer and make a difficult decision about redundancies.

'hard' and 'difficult' are very popular words but are they descriptive enough?

Are these words more meaningful?

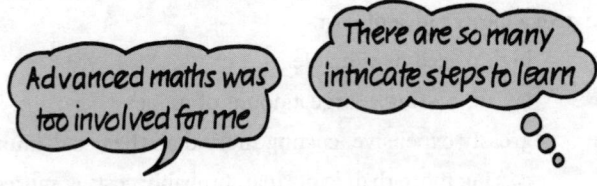

TUESDAY	FEBRUARY

I had a strenuous day at work. I had to complete several complex reports, deal with an obstreperous customer and make a painful decision about redundancies.

Which other words could be used?

arduous	intractable	onerous
laborious	unaccommodating	wearisome
obscure	formidable	problematical
perverse	perplexing	unamenable
tiresome	involved	troublesome

** An antonym for 'hard' and 'difficult' is 'easy'. Complete these additional antonyms.

s_m_le   unco_pl_ _at_ _

ef_ _ _tless   str_ _ _ _tfor_ _ _ _

un_ _man_ing   c_ _ar

ach_ _ _ble   at_ _ _ _able

dear

When we describe an item as being 'costly' or 'high in price', we often use the word 'dear'. While this is perfectly acceptable, there is a range of words which we could use to add variety to our conversation and writing. Such words can give a clearer idea of cost.

costly	high priced or valuable
expensive	lavish, costing a large amount of money
exorbitant	grossly expensive, costing more than the usual amount
excessive	costing more than is normal, probably costing more than it is worth paying
extortionate	too much money is demanded
overpriced	an item priced at more than its value

Helpful Hints

▶ 'Pricey' is colloquial and can only be used in informal conversation.

** 'Inexpensive' is the opposite of 'dear'. Complete these words which also mean 'inexpensive'.

ch_ _ _   bar_ _ _ _

reas_ _ _ _ _ _   affor_ _ _ _ _

eco_ _ _ _ _ _ _

'Dear' can also refer to people or items which are 'precious' to us.

EXAMPLES:

My aunt is very dear to me.

My mother's bracelet, which I inherited, is very dear to me.

** Use your thesaurus to find alternative words for 'dear' (meaning 'precious'). Arrange them in two lists: those suitable for describing people and those suitable for describing objects.

give up

EXAMPLES:

I'm giving up my job.

My brother's given up his girlfriend.

Our dentist is giving up tennis.

Can other words be used?

abandon	cease	capitulate
relinquish	cede	desist (from)
quit	resign	surrender
forswear	waive	

** Using words from the panel above, find which words can replace those underlined below.

1 He had to <u>give up</u> all thoughts of a career in the police force when he failed his medical.

2 The small band of rebels was forced to <u>give up</u>.

3 It was time to <u>give up</u> his commission in the army.

4 Rachel decided to <u>give up</u> her place in the team to a younger player.

5 If you do not <u>give up</u> interfering, you will be sacked.

6 Placing his hand on the Bible, he swore that he would <u>give up</u> his criminal practices.

give out

** Use your thesaurus to find alternative words for:

'Give out' when it means 'discharge'.

e.g. The toxic waste gave out/discharged huge quantities of poisonous gases into the surrounding countryside.

'Give out' when it means 'to make known'.

e.g. The district councillor gave out that she would be retiring in June.

Final thoughts

Whenever you are speaking or writing, consider your audience and the situation. **Formal situations require formal vocabulary.**

Although we are not suggesting that you change your way of speaking or avoid conversational words altogether, it is a good idea to practise using a wide range of words both in speaking and writing.

9
Faded Words

In this chapter we will be looking at words which, whilst they are not colloquial, are used so frequently in everyday speech and writing that their meanings have become blunted. Such words, which no longer afford us a clear picture, can be replaced by more interesting words. This chapter introduces you to the possibilities and encourages you to use a more varied vocabulary.

Overused words

nice

nasty

good

bad

strange

big or large and little or small

old and young

interesting

rich and poor

like and don't like

get and got

nice

EXAMPLES:

It's a nice village.

She always looks nice.

Alice wore a nice dress.

You will hear comments like this every day; they are part of our natural conversation. Although we understand all of these comments, they are bland, vague statements which give us little information. Other words could have been used.

EXAMPLES:

It's an attractive village.

She always looks glamorous

Alice wore a pretty dress.

Why is it 'nice'?

I had a nice holiday.	I had a relaxing holiday.
She is nice.	She is understanding
Your garden is nice.	Your garden is colourful

By replacing the word 'nice' we have more interesting and precise information about the holiday, person and garden.

In writing, we may try to be even more exact and descriptive, using additional words to replace 'nice'.

EXAMPLE:

I had a quiet and relaxing holiday.

She is understanding and sympathetic.

Your garden is well-planned and colourful.

'lovely' and 'beautiful'

These words are used in the same way as 'nice' to mean 'very pleasing' or 'delightful'.

EXAMPLES:

Alternative words

There is a range of synonyms which can be used according to the degree of 'delight' we wish to express.

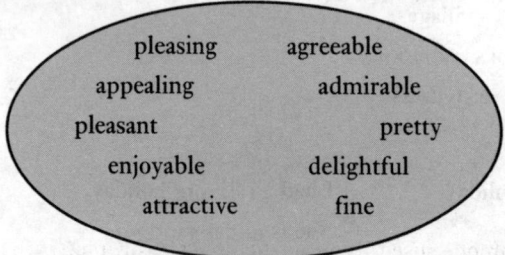

pleasing   agreeable
appealing   admirable
pleasant   pretty
enjoyable   delightful
attractive   fine

In other situations you may wish to use words which explain why someone or something is nice, lovely or beautiful.

e.g. My boss is nice.

Do you like him because he is

well-mannered?	kind?
generous?	amiable?
thoughtful?	friendly?
warm-hearted?	amusing?

e.g. This is a nice room.

Do you approve of it because it is

tidy?	neat?
large?	well-furnished?
modern?	airy?

** Use your thesaurus to help you find a range of words to describe each of these situations.

1 a nice child (He is well-mannered.)

2 a nice essay (It is accurate.)

3 a nice face

4 a nice dress

** Complete these words, all of which express a very high degree of approval or satisfaction with someone or something. You may need to refer to your thesaurus.

```
g_ _g_ _ _ _        exq_ _ _ _ _ _
cap_ _v_ _ _ _ _     eng_ _ _ _ _
grat_ _ _ _ _ _      all_ _ _ _ _
app_ _l_ _ _         wi_ _ _ _g
r_d_ _ _t            rav_ _ _ _ _ _
```

nasty

'Nasty' is commonly used to mean the opposite of 'nice'. It is an overused word, used for a variety of diverse situations.

> **nasty** näs'ti adj. disgustingly foul: obscene: threatening:
> ill-natured: difficult to deal with: unpleasant

In everyday speech and writing it is mostly used in its mildest form meaning 'unpleasant'.

EXAMPLES:

Don't be nasty!

I have a nasty cold.

The weather is nasty today.

What a nasty smell!

** 'Nasty' can mean the opposite of nice, lovely or beautiful. Go back to the key word 'nice', look through the suggestions for alternative words and see which words can have a prefix added to them to become synonyms for 'nasty'.

e.g. pleasant   unpleasant

Alternatives to nasty

disgusting	improper
*lewd	*malodorous
sickening	offensive
nauseating	*odious
revolting	*repugnant
*noisome	unappetizing
polluted	obscene
*repellent	foul
vile	*despicable

*loathsome	indecent
ill-natured	*unsavoury
*obnoxious	*surly
*vicious	unkind
*malicious	spiteful

** Use your dictionary to check the definitions of any words from the lists above that you are uncertain of, then write a simple definition of each word from memory.

** Using words from those shown above, make a list of the most suitable words to describe each situation.

1 nasty weather

2 nasty smell

3 nasty taste (food)

4 nasty temper

5 nasty language

6 nasty pool of stagnant water (industrial waste)

---

good

Someone or something having desirable or suitable qualities is often described as 'good'. It is sometimes used in the same way as 'nice', e.g. 'I had a good holiday', so some of the words listed under 'nice' can also be used to replace 'good'.

EXAMPLES:

admirable   agreeable   pleasant   pleasing

Replacing 'good'

'Good' is used for so many situations that there is a rich supply of alternative words.

e.g. Paul Pearson is a good doctor.

Perhaps he is:

adept	kind
accomplished	competent
trustworthy	helpful
talented	skilful
efficient	proficient
reliable	clever

e.g. Melissa obtained good results in her examinations. Were they:

satisfactory?	first-class?
exemplary?	excellent?
praiseworthy?	commendable?

e.g. Teresa Holmes, our receptionist, is a good person. Is she considered to be:

honest?	upright?	virtuous?
friendly?	humane?	dependable?
kind-hearted?	genuine?	trustworthy?

** Use a dictionary and a thesaurus to find suitable words to use instead of 'good' in these situations.

1 good weather

2 good food

3 good student (producing good work)

4 good bracelet (costly)

5 good decision (He was praised for making it.)

6 good crop of strawberries

▶ We use the expression 'for your own good'.

e.g. I am telling you for your own good.

In this expression 'good' is used as a noun.

** Use your thesaurus to find suitable replacement words for 'good' when it is used as a noun.

bad

This is an antonym for 'good' and, like 'good', it is very widely used.

e.g. It is a bad car – I am always sending it to the garage to be repaired.

The car could be described as:

faulty	imperfect	defective
inferior	substandard	unsatisfactory

e.g. Most of the villagers considered Alf to be a bad person.

Alf was possibly:

wicked   corrupt   criminal   base   evil

immoral   villainous

** Use your thesaurus to make a list of suitable words to replace 'bad' in each of these sentences.

1 Even Lee's friends described him as a <u>bad</u> boy because he was always being punished for his misdeeds.

2 On their return, they discovered that the food in the faulty refrigerator was <u>bad</u>.

3 Their <u>bad</u> financial position had been caused by the recession.

4 I feel <u>bad</u> about your house being broken into when I was supposed to be looking after it.

5 Phil Thomas has chronic asthma and was unable to attend the committee meeting because he was <u>bad</u>.

Helpful Hints

▶ 'Awful' is often used to show that someone or something is very bad.

e.g. I had an awful headache.

▶ 'Awful' also means:

tiresome

inspiring fear, dread or wonder

It is used colloquially to mean 'very' or 'great'.

EXAMPLES:

I don't want an awful lot. (great)

The video was awfully amusing. (very)

Avoid using 'awful' and 'awfully' in this way.

▶ 'not bad'

He's not bad   That cake's not bad

We use 'not bad' to show that someone or something is:

| adequate | acceptable | sufficient | average |
| fair | passable | moderate | tolerable |

'Not bad' is a conversational phrase and should not be used in formal writing.

strange

'Strange' means:

    alien

    not previously known or experienced

    unfamiliar

    interestingly unusual

We often resort to using 'strange' when someone or something puzzles us and we cannot think of another word to use.

e.g. The groom had a strange expression as he emerged from the stables.

Was his expression:

    puzzling?

    enigmatic?

    curious?

    peculiar?

    perplexing?

e.g. The conductor was renowned for his strange clothes and behaviour.

Were his clothes:

    bizarre?

    eccentric?

    exceptional?

    extraordinary?

You will notice that in some instances 'strange' is used in a similar way to 'funny' (see Chapter 8).

Replacing 'strange'

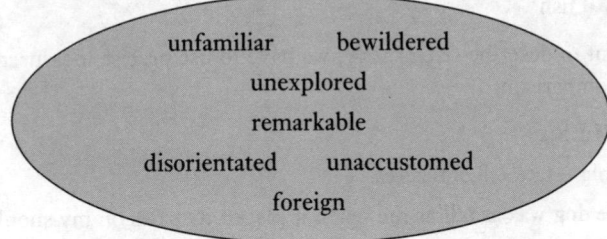

unfamiliar   bewildered

unexplored

remarkable

disorientated   unaccustomed

foreign

** Using each word from the circle once, replace 'strange' in each of these sentences.

1 My cousin is looking forward to visiting a <u>strange</u> country.

2 Braithwaite rarely scored many runs on a <u>strange</u> pitch.

3 She felt <u>strange</u> and uncertain of what to do.

4 I am <u>strange</u> to this department.

5 The boy scout felt <u>strange</u> – he had lost his sense of direction.

6 The plan was to visit <u>strange</u> parts of the jungle.

7 His <u>strange</u> powers impressed his audience.

abnormal	astonishing	awkward	irregular	mystifying
singular	unaccountable	weird	uncommon	foreign
exotic	new	novel	unknown	untried

** Each of the words in this panel could be used to replace 'strange' in a particular situation. Fit each word to a situation.

e.g. strange behaviour   abnormal behaviour

big or large and little or small

Size

Size is always difficult to describe as each of us has a different perception of:

a big estate

a large dog

a little piece

a small fish

If we want to describe size exactly, we have to use precise measurements or make a comparison.

EXAMPLES:

It was a big estate – 9,500 acres.

The large dog was as tall as me when it placed its paws on my shoulders.

I only want a little piece – half the size of Mary's slice.

He caught a small fish weighing only two pounds.

Age

'Big', 'little' and 'small' can also be used to describe someone's age.

EXAMPLES:

When I am big I want to be a mountaineer. (grown-up, mature, adult)

Claris was only little – two years old – when her brother was born.

As a small child, under the age of five, I was frightened of darkness.

Using other words

If we don't want to give precise ages or measurements or make comparisons, there is a range of words which can be used instead of 'big', 'little' and 'small'.

big or large

mammoth	extensive	colossal	enormous	immense
huge	massive	sizable	important	considerable
abundant	significant	leading	valuable	influential
powerful	vast	substantial	ample	bulky
burly	mature	plentiful	spacious	roomy

** Select appropriate words from the list above which could be used in each of these instances.

1 a large yield

2 a large house

3 a big parcel (heavy, irregularly shaped)

4 a big man (heavy, well-built)

5 a big statesman

6 a large inheritance

** These words can also be used in certain circumstances to replace 'big' or 'large'. Check their definitions in your dictionary.

voluminous	ponderous
paramount	prodigious
prominent	magnanimous

little or small

diminutive	unpretentious	miniature
minute	petite	immature
limited	meagre	scanty

** Extend this list by completing the words below.

tri_ _ _ _   unim_ _ _ _ _ _ _

negl_ _ _ _ _ _   insig_ _ _ _ _ _ _ _

inade_ _ _ _ _   insuf_ _ _ _ _ _ _

old and young

In the same way as 'big', 'small' and 'little' present only a vague notion about a person's age; so do the words 'old' and 'young'. Our judgements about 'old' or 'young' are often made in relation to our own ages.

EXAMPLES:

Her father was old – he had been forty when she was born.

The students seemed so young – younger than her own grown-up children.

If we are to be precise about age, we have to quote an exact figure. However, it is not always possible to be exact about the age of a person or object and then we need to use a range of words to make our speech and writing interesting.

old

ancient	used	antique	archaic
aged	worn	*decrepit	*antiquated
*obsolete	*dilapidated	*venerable	outdated
old-fashioned	stale	timeworn	*outmoded

** Use your dictionary to check the definition of each word above that has an asterisk beside it, then use each word in an interesting sentence of your own.

young

** Complete each word from the clue given. Each answer is associated with 'young' or 'youthful'.

1 A child aged seven or younger   i_ _ _ _ _

2 Between a child and an adult   a_ _ _ _ _ _ _ _ _

3 A young person who is not mature   i_ _ _ _ _ _ _

4 Behaving in a childish way   j_ _ _ _ _ _ _

5 School for children aged 7-11   j_ _ _ _ _

6 A young bird   f_ _ _ _ _ _ _

7 Behaviour unsuited to an adult   c_ _ _ _ _ _ _

8 Behaving like a very young child   i_ _ _ _ _ _ _

9 Childish or silly   p_ _ _ _ _ _

---

interesting

EXAMPLES:

Mull is an interesting island to visit.

An Inspector Calls is an interesting play.

Rosa is an interesting person.

Elizabeth finds her new job most interesting.

> **interesting** means 'engaging the attention' or 'exciting emotion or passion'.

What are the alternatives?

captivating	engrossing	intriguing	absorbing
inspiring	riveting	fascinating	stimulating
diverting	exciting	spell-binding	thought-provoking
entertaining	amusing	appealing	unusual
provocative	gripping	engaging	compelling

** Select one or more of the words above to suit each of these situations.

1 an interesting television programme that made you think about the subject afterwards

2 an interesting book which aroused your curiosity

3 an interesting film which captured your attention entirely

4 an interesting play – full of suspense and drama

5 an interesting pantomime – all the children were quiet and completely attentive

6 an interesting comment which was designed to make people debate the issue

** Make a list of antonyms for 'interesting'.

rich and poor

rich

'Rich' means more than being wealthy or having abundant possessions.

A country can be rich in natural resources.

Rich soil is fertile and productive.

A deep colour is a rich colour.

A rich sound is full-toned.

A rich taste is full-flavoured.

A rich food may abound with fat, sugar, oil, fruit, eggs, cream, etc.

A person whose life is rich may not possess great wealth but life may be rich in other ways – in friendship, culture and self-fulfilment.

What other words could be used?

productive	luxuriant	flavoursome	luxurious
prosperous	fruitful	creamy	lavish
deep	delicious	affluent	juicy
copious	lush	mellow	full
resonant	sumptuous	succulent	fertile
tasty	opulent	ample	wealthy
abundant	plentiful	warm	strong
	bright	vivid	

** Use the words above to find the following.

1 Two words which mean 'costly-looking' and 'splendid'.

2 Which word means 'generous' and perhaps 'wasteful with money'?

3 Which words can be used to describe a person with plenty of money?

4 Choose three words to describe soil which is rich.

5 A <u>rich</u> yield of grapes could be described by which two words?

6 Which two words would you choose to describe a dense, green lawn?

7 Choose six words which could describe <u>rich</u> food.

8 Find five words to describe a <u>rich</u> colour.

9 Which words could be used to describe a <u>rich</u> sound?

poor

'Poor' is an antonym for 'rich'.

impecunious	poverty-stricken	substandard
wretched	scanty	insufficient
inferior	deficient	paltry
destitute	unproductive	impoverished
inadequate	unsatisfactory	faulty
needy	infertile	penniless

According to the situation, these words can all be used to replace 'poor'.

** Find the most suitable words for each situation below.

1 poor – with little money

2 poor soil

3 poor supply of food

4 poor quality

like and don't like

All the previous key words in this chapter can be used as adjectives, describing or giving more information about nouns. The remaining key words in this chapter are verbs.

like

'like' is a verb meaning:

to enjoy

to approve of

to be pleased with

It is a word we use very frequently.

Choosing more interesting words

take pleasure in	approve of
cherish	appreciate
hold dear	love
prize	enjoy
esteem	relish
revel in	admire
delight in	be partial to
be fond of	

Helpful Hints

'Love' means to regard with affection or to be fond of.

'Adore' means to love intensely or to worship.

Both words are stronger in meaning than 'like' and should not be overused or applied in an exaggerated way.

don't like

When we want to express our dislike of someone or something, we may choose to use the words 'don't like'.

If we wish to express a stronger degree of dislike, we may use verbs such as:

hate	detest	despise	execrate	loathe	abhor	abominate

or

be hostile to	recoil from
have an aversion to	be repelled by

** Check the meaning of any words from the panels above that you are uncertain about, then write an interesting sentence for each verb.

e.g. I have an aversion to snakes and cannot even bear to look at photographs of them.

** 'Hate' is a verb but 'hatred' is a noun. Change as many as possible of the verbs in the panels into nouns. Use your thesaurus to find additional nouns which mean the same as 'hatred'.

got and get

EXAMPLES:

I get up at 8 am.

Sharma gets her eggs at the farm.

Rory got bitten by a dog.

These two words can occur with monotonous regularity in our speech and informal writing. They should be avoided in formal situations.

Get and got are used in many different ways.

EXAMPLES:

get a reputation for	(acquire)
get old	(become)
get a coat	(fetch)
get a present	(receive)
get the meaning of	(understand)
get a meal	(prepare)

Avoiding 'get' and 'got'

There is an abundance of words that you can choose to replace 'get' and 'got' according to the context in which each is used.

arise	procure	overcome	attain
develop	comprehend	arise	coax
arrive at	make ready	take in	prosper
inherit	arrange	become infected	survive
alight	appropriate	induce	secure
contract	convince	succeed	reach

fall victim to	communicate with	be afflicted with	fathom
enter	obtain	disembark	earn
carry	influence	gain	contrive
urge	follow	receive	benefit
arrest	fix	recover	grow
persuade	take	approach	perceive
seize	win	contact	manage

** Choose an appropriate word to replace the underlined word or words in each of these sentences. You can use words from the list but you will also need to think of additional replacement words.

1 Shirley got top marks in her swimming examination.

2 My neighbour got first prize for her roses.

3 I have got the answer to the problem.

4 My sister has got a yacht and a dinghy.

5 Sybil's brother got malaria when he was in Africa.

6 Will you get the children from school for me?

7 He got into a fight on Saturday.

8 The teenager got on his bike and got away.

9 I will go to the library to get a book about Dryden.

10 Joan's mother can usually get her to mow the lawn.

11 As you get to the church, it is on your right.

12 The coach will get to Manchester at 15.30.

13 If you work hard, you will get what you want.

14 My father got a considerable amount of money when his aunt died.

15 If you can get over the initial feeling of nausea, you will enjoy the experience.

Colloquial phrases

'Got' and 'get' are used in a number of colloquial phrases.

** As colloquial words and phrases should be avoided in formal writing and speech, consider how you can rewrite the phrases below.

1 I can get by with just a few words of Italian.

2 February always gets me down.

3 My son has always been able to <u>get in on</u> any party or outing.

4 If only I could <u>get across</u> my feelings to my father.

5 My grandmother has plenty of <u>get-up-and-go</u> for her age.

6 Maria felt he was always <u>getting at</u> her.

You can't expect to remember the precise meanings of all the words in this chapter so be prepared to go back from time to time and check up on words. It is only with practice that you will extend your vocabulary and use a variety of words confidently instead of always resorting to the same familiar 'faded' words.

9

10
Shades of Meaning

If you were an artist and attempted to paint a picture of a landscape using merely the primary colours, you would not be successful in capturing the scene. An artist needs to use shades of each primary colour to reproduce the scene accurately. Similarly, if a writer wishes his reader to have a clear view of the subject, **he must select the most apt and descriptive words to express his ideas and observations. Only then will the exact meaning be conveyed accurately.**

In this chapter you will be introduced to a number of key words. Each key word is perfectly acceptable to use, but there are other words which are similar in meaning and are often more suited to a specific situation. We hope this chapter:

▶ makes you more aware of the wealth of choice at your disposal;

▶ encourages you to select the best word for the situation;

▶ helps you to avoid using a word so frequently in a piece of writing that it becomes tedious and repetitive.

Key words

quiet

happy

cold

empty

full

heavy

bright

dull

fat and thin

careful

careless

quiet

EXAMPLES:

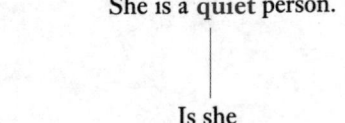

She is a quiet person.

Is she

modest?   reserved?   even-tempered?

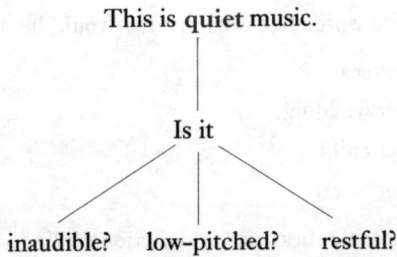

This is quiet music.

Is it

inaudible?   low-pitched?   restful?

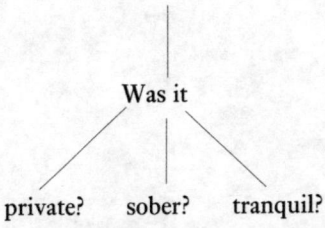

It was a quiet occasion.

Was it

private?   sober?   tranquil?

We use 'quiet' for so many situations that at times it neither expresses our ideas exactly nor does it create a vivid picture.

Which of these two sentences is more effective?

He walked quietly through the quiet building.

He walked noiselessly through the silent, peaceful building.

Reading the second sentence, we begin to feel the stillness and tranquillity of the scene – 'quietly' and 'quiet' fail to convey the depth of the silence.

Alternatives to quiet

hushed	subdued	meek
shy	contented	gentle
soundless	calm	serene
unpretentious	collected	docile
retiring	motionless	smooth
secret	unobtrusive	conservative
imperturbable	sedate	isolated
undisturbed	plain	restrained
mild	simple	untroubled

** Choose words from this list that could be used to describe:

1 a quiet sea
2 a quiet wedding
3 a quiet child
4 a quiet wood

** Using your thesaurus and dictionary find suitable antonyms for 'quiet' that could describe:

1 a rough sea
2 someone's lively personality
3 flamboyant clothing
4 a noisy city

happy

'Happy' is used to convey a range of emotions from contentment to elation.

EXAMPLES:

Sarah was **happy** when her baby was born.

Mike walked along the road, **happy** to be out in the fresh air once more after his long day at work.

I was **happy** to be awarded first prize.

The **happy** civilians waved to the soldiers who had liberated their town.

The children's **happy** laughter showed their enjoyment of the puppet show.

** Consider these words which can be used as alternatives to 'happy'. For each situation described in the examples opposite, choose words that describe the emotion more precisely.

gratified	joyous	pleased
glad	merry	blissful
blithe	thrilled	content
cheerful	jubilant	overjoyed
ecstatic	elated	delighted

** What is meant by these conversational phrases?

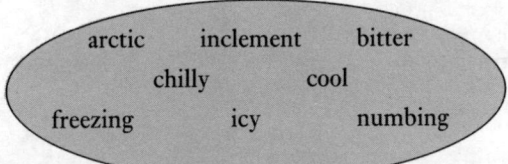

happy-go-lucky   a **happy** event

a **happy** medium   a **happy** hunting-ground

slap **happy**

** Complete these words which are all antonyms of 'happy'.

f _ _ _or _   s _ _br_   m_l_n _ _ o _y

de_ _ _on_e _t   m_s _ _a _le   m _ur_f _l

cold

The word 'cold' is frequently used to describe the weather but how 'cold' is 'cold weather'?

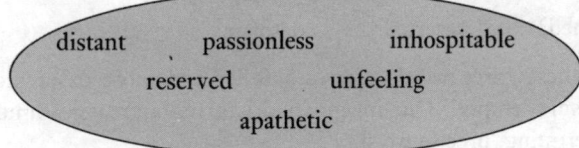

arctic   inclement   bitter

chilly   cool

freezing   icy   numbing

We sometimes hear people described as 'having a cold manner', but what is a 'cold' manner?

distant   passionless   inhospitable

reserved   unfeeling

apathetic

A clearer picture is created if we are given a word that indicates more precisely the degree of coldness or the exact nature of the person.

bleak	biting
indifferent	aloof
phlegmatic	unresponsive
raw	frosty
frigid	undemonstrative
glacial	wintry

** Sort the words from the panel into two lists: those that can be used to describe people and those we can use for the weather. Some words may be used for both situations.

** Using a thesaurus and a dictionary, find words and phrases to describe how cold you may feel on a winter's day.

If a cold person is regarded as being passionless, a person with a warm personality may be described as passionate.

** Complete these words that may also be used to describe a passionate person.

f_ _ry	an_m_t_d
e_ _ti_ _al	v_ _al
imp_ _uo_s	i_pu_si_e

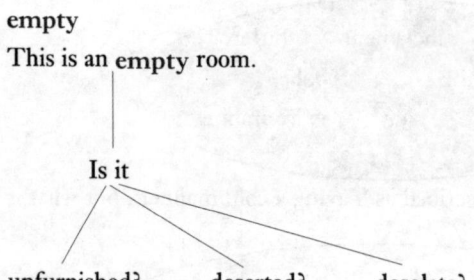

empty

This is an empty room.

Is it

unfurnished?   deserted?   desolate?

Each of these three words creates a fuller and more exact picture than merely using 'empty'. Our imagination is given a greater stimulus by the more interesting, precise word.

It was an empty promise.

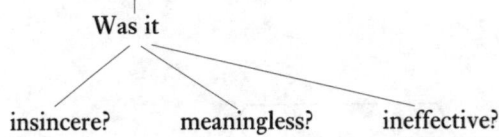

insincere?   meaningless?   ineffective?

Each of these three words conveys a subtle difference that may be absent in the less expressive word 'empty'. When writing, 'empty' is often the first word we select to describe:

nothing within

a lack of occupation

lacking substance

It may be the correct or only word to use in some instances, but there are alternatives which may convey your ideas more accurately.

hollow	aimless	vacant
uninhibited	bare	void
vacuous	inane	purposeless
absent	worthless	idle
futile	trivial	senseless
banal	unintelligent	blank

** Select one of the above alternatives to complete each of the following sentences.

1 Rodney reviewed his .... life and regretted the wasted opportunities.

2 The children, having removed all the decorations, surveyed the .... room.

3 The .... countryside looked bleak in the cold winter light.

4 A .... gesture is not worth making.

5 She sat looking at the .... paper, willing herself to write.

The alternative words for 'empty' that you have already encountered have been used as adjectives, but 'empty' may also be used as a verb.

** Complete these words, all of which can be used as alternatives to the verb 'empty'.

c_ns_m_   v_ _at_   ev_ _ua_ _

d_ _in   d_ _l_te   e_h_u_t

full

Full (adjective)
containing all it can hold
crowded
supplied with
complete
roomy
deep

We might say:

My glass is full.

Sue wore a full skirt.

The shelves held a full range of goods.

There are many interesting and precise words that more clearly express the various shades of meaning of 'full'.

My glass is brimming.

Sue wore a voluminous skirt.

The shelves held a comprehensive range of goods.

Other alternatives:

copious	entire	capacious
ample	resonant	saturated
crammed	detailed	rounded
plentiful	extensive	complete
loose	generous	abundant
voluptuous	gorged	exhaustive

** Choose one of the words from the list above to replace 'full' in each of these sentences. You may need to alter the wording of the sentence.

1 The towel was <u>full of</u> water.
2 His <u>full</u> knowledge of Africa proved useful when they visited Zambia.
3 Her <u>full</u> figure caused problems when she tried to buy the latest fashions.
4 The <u>full</u> crop of plums broke the tree's branches.
5 The student's <u>full</u> notes helped him when it was time to revise.

'Full-up' is a colloquial expression which we may use to show we have eaten enough.

More formally we could use:

replete

satisfied

satiated

** What do these expressions mean?

full-blooded	full-scale
fully fitted	full face
full-bodied	fully fledged
fulsome	a full house

heavy

'Heavy' is used in many ways.

EXAMPLES:

The parcel was too **heavy** to carry.

The boat was tossed about on the **heavy** sea.

She finds *The Times* too **heavy** and prefers the *Daily Express* because it is quicker to read.

The **heavy** traffic prevented me from arriving on time.

The tree was **heavy** with fruit.

He was a **heavy** burden on the family.

The **heavy** sky gave warning of bad weather.

My work load is too **heavy** for me to be able to commit myself further.

He awoke and lay motionless, his body still **heavy** with sleep.

Alternatives to 'heavy'

a heavy parcel	(weighty, bulky, hefty)
a heavy sea	(rough, tempestuous, turbulent, violent)
a heavy newspaper	(difficult, tedious, complex, deep, profound, serious, weighty)
heavy traffic	(excessive, considerable)
heavy with fruit	(laden, loaded, weighted)
a heavy burden	(intolerable, severe, wearisome)
a heavy sky	(oppressive, gloomy, glowering, stormy, leaden, louring)
a heavy work load	(oppressive, tedious, onerous)
heavy with sleep	(drowsy, torpid, sluggish, listless)

As you can see, there are many words that can be used instead of 'heavy' to give a more distinct and vivid picture.

Additional alternatives to 'heavy'

harsh	gloomy	boisterous
encumbered	inert	profuse
portly	ponderous	solemn

If any of the alternatives are unfamiliar, check their meanings in a dictionary.

** Match each adjective to the appropriate noun.

adjective	noun
onerous	body
solemn	footsteps
profuse	responsibility
oppressive	bleeding
inert	heat
ponderous	occasion

** The following words are antonyms for 'heavy'. Complete each word by writing in the missing letters.

s_igh_   t_ _v_ _l   sp_ _s_

a_ _le   c_l_   be_r_b_e

124

bright

'Bright' has been used above to describe:

someone's future

the weather

a child

a light

'Bright' means:

full of light

clear

clever

illustrious

vivid

With so many possible meanings, it is no wonder there is a variety of alternatives that we could use to describe situations more accurately.

blazing	astute	sunny
auspicious	cloudless	vivacious
dazzling	intense	radiant
cheerful	distinguished	promising
fair	ingenious	intelligent
favourable	lively	glorious
scintillating	propitious	brilliant
remarkable	lustrous	shimmering

** Look up in a dictionary any of the words above that you are uncertain of. Choose suitable words from the lists to describe more exactly the situations shown in the speech bubbles.

** Complete these words which can also be used instead of 'bright' in certain sentences.

l_m_no_s   s_a_t   o_tst_nd_ _g

g_ea_i_g   sp_ _k_ _ng   g_ _wi_g

dull

This is often used to convey the opposite of 'bright'. It also has a number of more descriptive and precise alternatives.

dismal	obscure	doleful
joyless	stupid	cheerless
gloomy	untalented	depressed
obtuse	monotonous	leaden
prosaic	drab	murky

** In each of these sentences, replace **dull** with a more exact word.

1 The <u>dull</u> weather over the holiday period caused many people to stay at home.

2 He awoke feeling <u>dull</u> and lethargic.

3 Without the customary glowing fire, the room looked <u>dull</u> and uninviting.

4 Winston had hoped to enjoy the party but the <u>dull</u> conversation made him leave early.

5 Listening to the others' achievements, she felt <u>dull</u> and inadequate.

fat and thin

'Fat' is often used to describe people or animals but is it sufficiently precise?

EXAMPLES:

Andrea is plump.

The mayor was corpulent.

Their dog was obese.

Each of the words underlined is describing a degree of 'fatness'.

plump, well filled out or rounded.

corpulent, physically bulky.

obese, grossly or abnormally fat – a medical term.

By choosing a word other than 'fat', we can more clearly show:

the size of the person;

our attitude towards the person and his or her size.

Other alternatives to 'fat'

rounded	rotund	gross
flabby	chubby	portly
ample	buxom	bulky
stout	paunchy	beefy
tubby	bouncing	brawny

** Choose words from the list which you would use to describe:

a fat baby

a fat businessman

If we were asked for the opposite of 'fat', we would probably answer 'thin' – but again this word lacks precision. More exact words for 'thin' are shown below.

scraggy	emaciated	slim
skeletal	slender	scrawny
spindly	lean	slight

** Some of these words are uncomplimentary. List those words you could use to present an unflattering picture of a person.

'Thin' is not only used to describe people. We also talk of:

thin material

thin hair

a **thin** excuse

a **thin** story

Other alternatives to 'thin'

sheer	scanty	diaphanous
sparse	flimsy	superficial
diluted	watery	transparent
insubstantial	wispy	transparent
unconvincing	inadequate	translucent

** From the list above, choose three words suitable to describe each of the following.

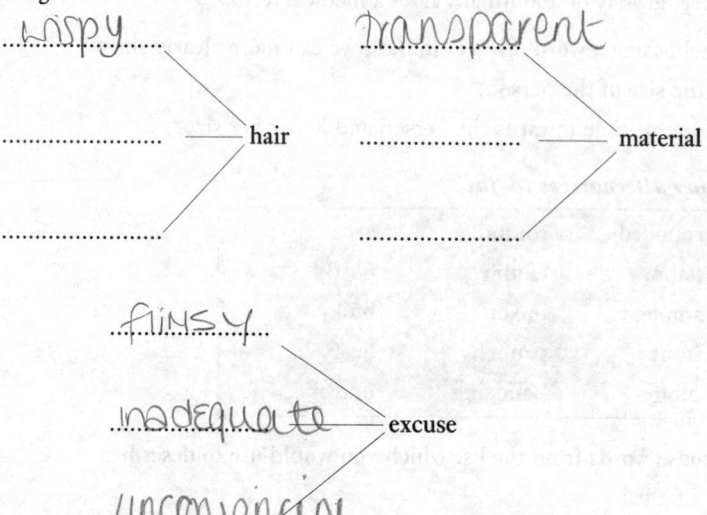

** What do these expressions mean?

a thin time	into thin air
thin on the ground	thin-skinned

careful

What is meant by 'careful' in each of these sentences?

Her **careful** writing was admired by everyone.

neat?   accurate?   painstaking?

Henry's parents were very careful.

cautious?   conscientious?   thrifty?

'Careful' can be used to express several different ideas: without being given any further information, we may be confused or fail to grasp the writer's exact meaning. 'Careful' may be defined as:

painstaking

watchful

cautious

Alternatives to 'careful'

attentive	precise	discreet
vigilant	concerned	fastidious
prudent	alert	particular

** Using the definitions to help you, complete these further examples of alternatives to 'careful'.

c_ _r_	wary or cautious in manner
p_nc_i_io_s	very careful about detail
_ee_ful	careful to take notice
sc_r_u_p_u_l_o_us	very conscientious
ju_d_i_ci_o_us	careful in making judgements
s_l_ _it_us	concerned, anxious

** Choose words to describe these people.

1 a **careful** driver

2 a person who is **careful** with his or her money

3 a person who is **careful** about his or her appearance

4 a person who is **careful** in his or her speech

5 a person who is **careful** about the safety of others

careless

'Careless' implies a lack of thought, but there is a difference between mere thoughtlessness that may offend and a thoughtless action that could endanger life. More exact words help to clarify the degree of carelessness and the seriousness of the situation.

EXAMPLES:

a **careless** remark (inconsiderate, indiscreet, perfunctory, thoughtless)

careless work (inaccurate, slapdash, negligent, hasty)

a **careless** manner (casual, nonchalant, unconcerned)

a **careless** person (absent-minded, unthinking, irresponsible)

** Match each of these definitions to one of the alternatives given above. Some of the letters of the word are already provided.

1 Undertaken from a sense of duty; or in a routine manner.   pe_ _u_ _t_ _ y

2 Showing a lack of anxiety; displaying no emotion.   no_ _ _a_an _

3 Imprudent; injudicious.   i_ _ _s_ _e_t

** By unscrambling these anagrams you will find other alternatives for 'careless'. In each case the first two letters of the unscrambled word is given.

orcursy	cu_ _ _ _ _
uadedrung	un_ _ _ _ _ _ _
tcgllufnee	ne_ _ _ _ _ _ _ _
tlessar	ar_ _ _ _ _
ldsseeeh	he_ _ _ _ _ _
indlufmun	un_ _ _ _ _ _ _
anhdoff	of_ _ _ _ _
diedtusnu	un_ _ _ _ _ _ _
soucianitu	in_ _ _ _ _ _ _ _

** Choose a suitable word to replace **careless** in each of these sentences.

1 Service at that restaurant is always **careless**.

2 His **careless** question caused her great distress

3 The **careless** repair to the car only held for a few miles.

4 The driver gave a **careless** glance in his mirror before driving away.

5 James was **careless** about his appearance.

Final thoughts

We hope this section has encouraged you to express your ideas exactly and vividly. You will find that it takes time to choose right word, the word which precisely conveys your ideas. At first, this may mean that you take longer to complete a piece of writing, but you will gradually extend your vocabulary and your search for the right word will become easier. As English is such a rich and varied language, it is foolish to restrict ourselves to using only the most obvious and commonplace words.

In Section 3 you will be given an opportunity to use a wide variety of words in creative and formal writing tasks.

10

11
Vivid Writing

There are many occasions when we try to use words effectively to create a colourful image, in, for example:

informal letters

essays

personal writing

Whatever the occasion, our intention is to describe our feelings or experiences accurately or give interest and enjoyment to our audience.

We have already seen in Section 2 that by choosing vivid and precise words we are more likely to be successful in describing people and situations. There will also be times when careful choice of descriptive words can make our formal writing more forceful or persuasive.

This chapter enables you to practise writing short passages based on a variety of situations or themes. The writing tasks have been carefully chosen to encourage you to write briefly but expressively as we have found that short passages are more likely to produce a 'sharply-etched' response than longer essays. The situations require different writing styles and language: descriptive and informative. For each situation a selection of relevant words is given, together with an example passage which shows how some of the words may be used.

Compare these two descriptions (taken from letters of complaint) about the same hotel.

When I arrived, I was upset by the poor state of the rooms. The bedroom and bathroom were both dirty, as were the sheets and towels. It was also dusty everywhere. I don't think it had been cleaned properly since the previous occupants had left. I expect a higher standard of cleanliness than this.

> When I arrived I was disgusted by the appalling state of the rooms. They were filthy, with dirty sheets on the bed and grimy towels in the bathroom. The surfaces in both rooms were dusty and sticky; the floor was covered in a film of cement dust. It was obvious that the rooms had not been cleaned since the departure of the previous occupants. I am sure you will agree that the accommodation failed to reach an adequate standard of cleanliness and comfort.

The second, more detailed and descriptive complaint, gives a clearer account of the state of the accommodation and is more likely to achieve a satisfactory response.

The situations and themes considered are:

darkness

food and eating

the sea

secretive movements

conversation

people

rain

an interview

a fight

a journey

darkness

In the following passage the writer is trying to create the atmosphere of a dilapidated area in a city at night.

> The man strode hurriedly along the shadowy street. Around him, dim, dingy houses crowded together, their windows broken and paint peeling. He shivered. Between the houses, in dark alleyways, menacing shadows took shape. Peering anxiously ahead, he was relieved to see a distant light whose welcoming glow penetrated the surrounding gloom.

11

Words which could be used to describe such a scene include:

dingy	murky	shadowy
shady	unlit	sunless
dismal	dim	gloomy
drab	dusk	sombre
glowering	obscure	overcast
derelict	abandoned	deserted
forsaken	neglected	destroyed

** See if you can create a similar atmosphere by writing a passage about a young child lost in fog on a cold November evening. Some of the words listed above will enable you to describe the denseness of the fog. You may like to refer to page 120 in Chapter 10 for some alternative words for 'cold'. In your description, try to convey the child's fear; the following words may help you with this.

bewildered	helpless
forlorn	solitary
petrified	alarmed
menacing	terrified

food and eating

As eating good food is one of the pleasures of life, we often describe enjoyable meals. In the passage below, the guests have waited for some time for their meal. Appetizing smells have made them hungry and so when faced with the food they fall upon it with gusto.

> The table groaned under the weight of serving dishes piled high with pungent steaming curries, pearly white rice and crisp nan bread baked to perfection.
> The guests, who had waited impatiently as the appetizing aroma drifted across the room, were now able to satisfy their ravenous hunger. Rapidly, the delicious food was transferred to their plates. Their faces relaxed as the first few succulent mouthfuls filled the hollow emptiness of their stomachs.

** Write a diary entry describing a special meal that you had been looking forward to for some time. Remember to refer to your anticipation as well as your appreciation of the meal. Words that may help you to describe the various aspects of the meal are listed opposite.

appetising	delectable	delicious
savoury	luscious	piquant
spicy	exquisite	palatable
succulent	flavoursome	dainty
aroma	bouquet	ravenous
greedy	yearning	famished
voracious	craving	devour
chew	consume	munch
nibble	savour	honeyed
melting	wholesome	redolent

the sea

In this situation we are considering how to create a contrasting picture of the same scene. Compare these two lists of words which conjure up very different impressions of a seascape.

calm	stormy
tranquil	tempestuous
peaceful	turbulent
placid	wild
smooth	harsh
still	boisterous
idyllic	tumultuous
undisturbed	foam
ripple	lash
lap	surge

In this passage, the scene rapidly changes from one of peace and tranquillity to that of storm and turmoil.

> In the pale, early morning light the tranquil sea beckoned; small boats rocked rhythmically in the breeze. The young girl plunged eagerly into the smooth water.
> As she drew level with the headland, the sun disappeared behind threatening storm clouds. Waves, which had

previously lapped gently over her, began to surge angrily against her. Squally showers swept across the water, and stinging sheets of rain blurred her vision.

** Describe a boat journey, contrasting the boat's quiet, steady exit from the harbour with the sudden rough conditions of the open sea. You may like to use some of these words to describe the boat's motion and the movement of the sea.

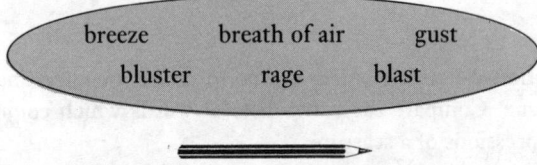

glide   roll   flow   buffet

drift   billow   swell

choppy   whirl   eddy   lurch

plunge   rock   pitch

Think also about the strength of the wind.

breeze   breath of air   gust

bluster   rage   blast

secretive movements

In essays you are sometimes asked to write about a situation from a particular point of view. Obviously you should try to focus your description accordingly. The following passage describes a cat's attempt to catch a bird. We follow the story first through the cat's and then the bird's actions.

> The emaciated cat stealthily stalked its unsuspecting victim. As the bird, sensing danger, nervously fluttered onto a nearby holly bush, the cat skulked under an adjoining shrub, casting surreptitious glances at its prey.
> The bird, perching tensely on a twig and ready for flight at any moment, issued a series of high-pitched warning cries. The cat pounced. The bird, in a frenzy of beating wings, tried to rise. For a moment it seemed as if the cat had succeeded: a flurry of feathers drifted down but the bird rose higher and now, safe from the cat's grasp, seemed to hover for a while before triumphantly circling and flying swiftly away.

Vocabulary

furtive   secretive   skulking

slinking	sly	stealthy
surreptitious	unseen	unsuspecting
conceal	disguise	muffle
sneak	prowl	stalk
creep	fluster	tremble

** Write a short description of an intruder creeping into a bedroom in which the occupant is asleep. Describe the actions of the intruder, the awakening of the occupant and how the intruder makes his escape.

conversation

> "I hate you," she shouted.
>
> "But why?" he queried.
>
> "Because you're a man," she replied, irrationally.
>
> "That isn't my fault," he snapped.
>
> "I know," she muttered, "but I hate you anyway."
>
> "Well, I don't know. Women are a mystery to me," he complained
>
> "That's because you're a man," she retorted.
>
> "That's it. I've had enough," he declared.

It is unlikely that you will write dialogue in letters or other everyday writing tasks, but you may include it in essays. Although you are unlikely to indicate who is speaking quite as often as we have in the example, there are times when you will have to show who is speaking. It becomes tedious to the reader if you constantly use 'said'; nor does 'said' give a clear picture of the way the words are spoken.

e.g. 'Come here,' he said.

A clearer picture is created by

> 'Come here,' he shouted.

gives the feeling of anger or urgency

or 'Come here,' he cajoled.

suggests gentle persuasion or even bribery.

▶ It is not only the words within the speech marks that paint a clear picture and create atmosphere but also the words that are chosen in place of 'said'.

In the previous dialogue a number of alternatives for 'said' were used. Other alternatives are:

inform	state	suggest
promise	explain	add
affirm	announce	assert
mention	remark	utter
disclose	claim	reason
repeat	ask	enquire
question	respond	answer
whisper	murmur	stammer
exclaim	puzzle	threaten

** Write a dialogue of a dispute in which a mother and daughter or son argue about clothes. Try to include a variety of words for 'said' which will help to describe the atmosphere.

people

Read this description of a brother and sister written by Barbara Pym in *Excellent Women*.

Julian Malory was about forty, a few years younger than his sister. Both were tall, thin and angular, but while this gave to Julian a suitable ascetic distinction, it only seemed to make Winifred, with her eager face and untidy grey hair, more awkward and gaunt. She was dressed, as usual, in an odd assortment of clothes, most of which had belonged to other people. It was well known that Winifred got most of her wardrobe from the garments sent to the parish jumble sales, for such money she had was never spent on herself but on Good – one could almost say Lost – Causes, in which she was an unselfish and tireless worker. The time left over from these good works was given to "making a home" for her brother, whom she adored, though she was completely undomesticated and went about it with more enthusiasm than skill.

By the end of the description, we have a clear idea of what Winifred looks like and some idea of her personality.

We are often asked to describe people: both their appearances and personalities. With an adequate supply of suitable words and an attention to detail, a reasonably accurate and vivid picture can be created.

Consider these details about a fictional character, Mr Ledgewick.

<u>His appearance</u> tall, lanky, lined face, sparse hair.

<u>His clothes</u> always wears the same black suit – threadbare, frayed, unfashionable.

<u>His manner</u> nervous, fidgety gestures, easily flustered, agitated and tense, talks very fast.

<u>His personality</u> excitable, friendly, benevolent, amiable, cordial, courteous, gentle, mild, lenient, indulgent, affable, genial.

** Select words from those listed above and write a detailed description of Mr Ledgewick.

rain

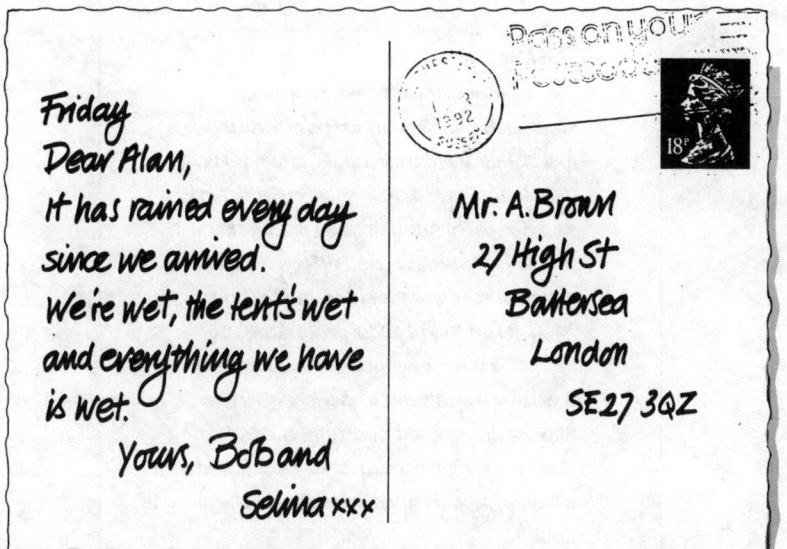

Living in Britain, we often have the opportunity to write about wet weather! Overleaf are some words we might use to describe a rainswept scene.

flood	deluge	torrent	drizzle	stream	teem
dank	drenched	dripping	saturated	waterlogged	clammy
humid	moist	sodden	soaked	sopping	soaking

We might want to describe an overcast sky using words such as those below.

pallid	cheerless	cloudy
dreary	leaden	threatening
livid	gloomy	wan

If you were describing Bob and Selina's holiday in a letter, you would probably choose a greater variety of words than 'wet' and 'rained'.

Hinstall Campsite,
Hinstall Farm,
Fordham,
Sussex
13th July 1992

Dear Alan,

We are sitting at the entrance of our tent surveying the scene: stretching out before us is a pallid grey sky which merges into a misty, dreary landscape. It is only drizzling at the moment but earlier this week we had several torrential downpours which soaked us and our tent. Our clothes are completely drenched and at night we squirm around in our sleeping bags trying to find the least sodden parts to lie on.

The campsite is surrounded by a wood which is probably very attractive at other times of the year. At present, walking in it is like entering a dank, clammy jungle with dripping leaves ready to send a trickle of icy water on you as you force your way through. . . .

** Write a description of a picnic which is spoilt by rain. Refer to the rising wind, clouds scurrying across the sky, the first few drops of rain, the frantic gathering-up of the picnic and the dash through heavy rain to the car.

---

an interview

The writer of this diary entry is trying to recapture her initial nervousness and anxiety, the impression created by the interviewers and her relief at the end of the ordeal.

SEPTEMBER · MONDAY

I went for my interview at Gleason's today. It was a nerve-racking experience. When my name was called I was shaking so much that I stumbled as I entered the office. Once inside, I was greeted by a row of four very solemn people who seemed to appraise me instantly and find me wanting before I had even answered a question. However, the personnel manager smiled at me reassuringly and offered me a seat (which was lower than the others in the room so the entire interview was conducted with me having to look up at my interviewers – a demeaning position).

I had great difficulty answering the questions at first; my mouth was so dry that my voice was either croaky or shrill and I didn't seem able to control it. They appeared to notice how nervous I was – my strained expression, intense concentration on their every word, tremulous voice – but the atmosphere gradually relaxed. By the end of the interview a feeling of euphoria swept over me as I gaily said goodbye and hurried from the room. I shall hear next week whether I was successful or not.

11

** Try writing the diary entry that one of the interviewers might have written about his or her experience of the same interview. Describe the interviewer's own feelings and impressions. Remember you will be considering the scene through another person's eyes and possibly a different picture will be created. These words may help you in your description.

tense	anxious
strained	agitated
apprehensive	fidgety
flustered	hesitant
ruffled	uneasy
quaking	shudder
intimidated	shiver

** Using the words below, write a brief description of an interview where the interviewee exudes confidence.

positive	self-assured
resolute	dauntless
fearless	self-reliant
firm	steady
calm	serene
collected	impassive
imperturbable	relaxed

a fight

So far in this chapter we have concentrated on using adjectives to create a descriptive passage. However, by using precise verbs you can describe movements exactly and so produce a colourful and accurate piece of writing. Compare these sentences.

The child **walked** along the deserted street.

The child **ambled** along the deserted street.

The child **trudged** along the deserted street.

The child **hurried** along the deserted street.

By choosing an alternative for 'walked', a more distinct impression is created.

Read this description of a playground fight. Notice the verbs that have been chosen to express the various actions.

> The circle of children closed around us, each child chanting, "Fight! Fight! Fight!" until the sound rang in my ears and, hitting out blindly, I landed the first punch. Jo darted away, bellowing with rage. Recovering, he hurled himself at me, pounding and battering me until I lost my footing and crashed to the ground where I lay, winded and dazed. Above me a sea of faces peered down, some concerned, others distorted with fury. Jo threw himself on top of me and we continued struggling until, worn out and drained of anger, we were separated.

** Using words from the passage and those listed below, write an account of a boxing or wrestling match. As well as describing the actions of the fighters, refer to the crowd, the noise and the fervent atmosphere.

punch	brawl	clash
tussle	resist	wrangle
bound	dash	spring
hurl	cuff	drag
scrape	scuffle	dodge
evade	roar	bawl
scream	thrilling	fervid
impassioned	stirred	heated
controversy	belligerent	combative

a journey

We frequently write letters or postcards to friends and relations when we are on holiday telling them about the places we have visited and the journeys we have undertaken. We want our audience to picture the scenes as we saw and experienced them, and derive similar pleasure and satisfaction from them.

In *Fat Man on a Bicycle*, Tom Vernon describes a cycle journey from London to the Mediterranean. He writes very amusingly about the journey and the diverse people he meets but he also describes the landscape with feeling and vivacity.

Where trees shaded the road, there were patches of coolness left over from the dawn, but the sun, though still low, was already hot. I passed an apple orchard where tall grasses were flowering with a pink fuzz in which the dew caught the light and broke it into a shower of glitters; then a paddock of rangy walnut trees. The road wound and wound; so did my legs, in bottom gear. My progress was slow but dignified, apart from a tendency to heavy breathing. I thought I had achieved something when I got to the top, and a nearby bird thought so too, for it broke into a fanfare of chirps: I attempted to record it, but the song was drowned in panting noises. The road curved round the side of the hill. I came to the crest of the last rise to see miles and miles of green Auvergne spread out before me, and a single lark above the wheat on my own hill-top.

In this next passage, Mark Wallington describes part of his walk around South West England.

Now, the sea grew agitated, the wind began to gust and the landscape lost all its finesse. You could feel Hartland Point long before you could see it.

On the map the promontory is a right angle, a corner where all the elements meet. In reality they collide, and the friction is frightening. The currents writhe in a vortex of grey water; the monstrous cliffs appear contorted under their own pressure and the waves hit them like trains. It's not a particularly attractive place, there's nothing subtle about it, it just looks mean.

We stood on the Point, above the lighthouse, as the cliffs groaned and Boogie's ears filled with the wind as though he might take off. And as we turned the corner and headed south you could see the coastline had changed. The round shoulders of Exmoor had gone; ahead lay jagged, weather-beaten cliffs of sandstone and shale. Even the plants were different; the woodlands had been replaced by a sparse table-top, and the vegetation was low and salt-encrusted. A squat, pink flower seemed to survive best and clumps of it grew in every crack in the rock. Otherwise only the gulls were at home here. They rose and fell on thermal elevators, harnessing the force of the wind rather than battling against it.

For the next three hours we hiked over this wild terrain, as banks of clouds mustered offshore and rode in on the Atlantic swell, and even the grass turned grey. The path was tough and steep, but the effort subconscious. I'd never seen cliffs like these before. The bedding planes were folded over each other, twisted and squashed, some were sliced clean and square as a cake, others were sharp as a broken bottle.

We climbed combe after combe, past Hartland Quay where a small hotel gazed nervously out to sea, past Speke's Mouth Mill, with its spectacular waterfall that tumbled over steps to the beach;

and as the light began to fail we finally climbed the last hill in Devon and saw Cornwall stretching away into the clouds. It was just headland after headland and we were going to have to climb every one of them.

(from 500 Mile Walkies)

This final extract is from an account of a hair-raising train journey through France and Italy.

As the train pulled out of Nice station just after 11pm last Friday there was an atmosphere of mild paranoia among the passengers. Most had heard about the robbery epidemic, and one American, who was travelling round Europe by train, had already fallen victim to the gangs. He was busy warning fellow travellers to jam their bunk ladders across the couchette doors. Some passengers followed his advice; others attempted to tie their doorhandles together with string or even sheets. Most, however, felt that locking the doors should be sufficient precaution. They were to be the unlucky ones.

As the train raced on, I noticed several young men hanging about the corridors of the first and second-class couchette compartments. I hoped that they might just be Interrailers from the seated carriages, waiting to use the superior washrooms of the first-class compartments.

My travelling companion and I stayed outside in the corridor until they had gone, and then went into our couchette, carefully locking the door behind us. We thought about putting the ladder in front of the door, but did not want to disturb the elderly Chinese couple sleeping below. At 6am we woke to find a young man standing in the couchette. His hand was on the handles of the Chinese woman's bag, which was at her feet. We shouted, and the thief ran out empty-handed. Then I realised that he had merely been coming back for more – our luggage, although we had tied it to the rack, had gone. We rushed out in hot pursuit, but the thief had vanished.

(from The European)

Write a description of a memorable journey you have undertaken. Consider the method of travel, the scenery and any fellow travellers. Try to recapture the atmosphere of the journey whether it was idyllic, tiring or disagreeable. The words listed below may suggest some ideas for your description.

drifting	arduous	challenging
disturbing	expectant	repetitious
unvaried	exhilarating	stimulating
prospect	alacrity	spectacular
distant	magnetism	intriguing
propitious	trepidation	indomitable
commotion	flurry	imposing
prominent	encroach	calamitous

In this chapter our main concern has been to encourage you to write descriptively, not only in essays but also in informal writing tasks. We hope it also shows that succinct and expressive vocabulary can improve spoken accounts and descriptions.

12
Being Formal

Formal versus informal

When we speak we adopt different tones of voice to reflect our moods and to accord with the formality of the situation. In writing we also have to pay attention to tone and know when to use a formal or informal style. Our reader or listener expects us to use a formal style and vocabulary for formal situations whereas the same style and vocabulary would be inappropriate for informal situations.

In many of the previous chapters we have advised you to avoid using certain words and phrases in formal speech and writing, as they may be too chatty for your intended audience or too imprecise for you to impart your message effectively.

The words you choose affect the formality of your message.

In this chapter we will consider:

> when to use formal language;
>
> words and phrases which are suited to formal situations.

When to use formal language

▶ When the situation is formal: for example an interview for a job or a letter to your bank.

▶ If you are speaking to or writing for a general audience: for example in a work situation – a letter to all customers, or a presentation to all staff.

▶ If the listener or reader is unknown to you: for example, a telephone enquiry in answer to an advertisement in a newspaper, or a letter of complaint to a manager of a store.

▶ If you want to pass on information or instructions which must be accurate. For example, explaining how to use a new piece of equipment to a colleague, or leaving details of a telephone message for a colleague.

Making the wrong choice

CRAVEN SUPPLIES
Unit 17a
Piddinghoe Industrial Estate
East Sussex
BN4 3EB
Tel: 0962 492904

December 17th 1992

Mrs E Flaherty
Bilston Chemicals
Reeve Lane
Chichester
West Sussex
PO4 197

Order Reference Number BM7R/294/172X

Dear Mrs Flaherty

Thanks for your letter. We got it yesterday. Our
new girl's dealing with it and you'll get it
soon. You know us — good service, prompt
delivery.

Don't forget, as usual, any problems or anything
I can do for you — just give us a bell.

As ever

P. Lomas

Pauline Lomas
Divisional Manager

Section 3

What impression do you gain of the firm and its divisional manager from
this letter? Is it:

12

informal?
relaxed?
friendly?
proud of its service?

Is the style and vocabulary appropriate for a letter to a customer?

This is a formal work situation.
Ms Lomas probably doesn't know
her customer personally.   A formal style is required.
She is providing a customer
with information.

** Look back at the letter and identify all the informal words and phrases and the unnecessary pieces of information. Rewrite the letter in the appropriate formal manner.

Read this transcript of a recorded message left on an Inland Revenue Department's answering machine.

> Bill Smithie here. I'd like the girl I had a natter with yesterday to ring me tomorrow. Don't know her name but she sounded a bit like my sister. Tell her I want a bit of info about Schedule D as I'm getting in a right muddle and the way I'm going I'll end up in Queer Street. I need an expert pronto. I'm sure she'll remember my number but here it is all the same — 69453.

What impression do you gain of the caller? Is he:

patronising?

disorganised?

impolite?

The woman dealing with Mr Smithie's tax affairs may well object to his informal, chatty, over-familiar style and feel less inclined to ring him back and offer her help. She might feel that his accounts need very careful scrutiny!

In both examples the writer and caller have used chatty, informal language unsuited to the situation and failed to consider their audiences, the tone of their messages and the degree of formality required. Their messages have lost their impact and effectiveness because of their misjudgement.

What is formal language?

Our speech and writing can tell people a great deal about us and perhaps this is why we sometimes feel inhibited about situations requiring formal speech or writing. As life becomes increasingly informal, the task of being formal becomes more difficult as we have less practice in our everyday lives. When we need to write a formal letter, attend an interview, give a vote of thanks, etc. we are anxious about being able to cope.

What should we say?

What words should we use?

Formal English should not be stilted and unnatural with an abundance of long words and complicated sentences; **it should be exact, precise, effective and fit its purpose and audience**.

Always consider

What is my purpose?

What do I want to achieve?

What is the best way of achieving my aim?

What is my audience?

Am I familiar with it?

What will it expect from me?

What might it be influenced by?

What is the appropriate tone to use?

Should I be formal or informal?

Should I be firm, conciliatory, persuasive, or . . .?

If you consider these points carefully, it will help you to select the words and phrases which are most useful to you and acceptable to your audience. By choosing the correct tone, degree of formality and vocabulary you should be successful.

If Bill Smithie had given greater consideration to his purpose, tone and audience, he might have said:

"This is Bill Smithie. My telephone number is 69453. I would be grateful if the officer I spoke to yesterday could telephone me tomorrow to give me some information about Schedule D."

By omitting irrelevant details and using a polite, conciliatory tone he has succeeded in leaving a brief but accurate message on the answering machine.

Selecting the right words

It is impossible to provide a definitive list of words which can be termed 'formal' as the words we use depend upon the particular situation, but listed below are *some* examples of formal words and phrases and their more informal equivalents.

informal	formal
come to (the meeting)	attend (the meeting)
write back	reply
do everything that is said (in the Data Protection Act)	comply with (the D.P.A.)
it's my job to . . .	it is my responsibility to . . .
to make sure (the customers) are all right	to safeguard (the customers)
the person or company you work for	employer
take off	remove
I have joined it to the letter	I have attached it
cross out the bits that aren't needed	delete as appropriate
arranged in order of date	arranged chronologically
roughly	approximately
the person who is applying for the job	the applicant
taken into (hospital)	admitted to
(rights) set down by law	statutory (rights)
the form you've filled in	completed form
to take as much care as you can	to take all reasonable care
sort out everything for you	arrange
extras which you don't have to have	optional extras
parts that aren't working properly	defective parts
listed on the back of this page	listed overleaf
worked quite all right	worked satisfactorily
(the manufacturer) says it's best to	recommends

causes me a lot of bother	is inconvenient
the house didn't have people in it	was unoccupied.
an instructor who's passed his exams	qualified instructor

You will notice that formal terms often require fewer words. In your endeavours to use formal language, don't overdo it. Formal English isn't wordy and cumbersome but simple, brief and straightforward.

EXAMPLES:

wordy	straightforward
I will acquaint you with all the facts as these may assist you in your decision.	I will give you all the facts as these may help you to decide.
My residence is situated in close proximity to the railway station.	My house is near the railway station.
The availability of cog wheels is now severely restricted.	There are few cog wheels in stock.

Formal speech

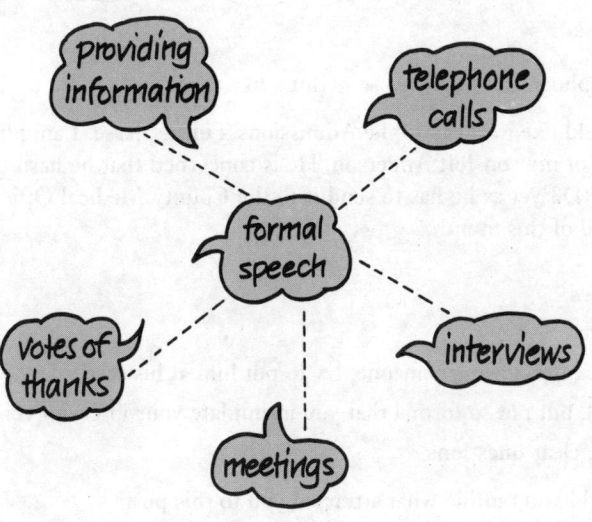

Whenever possible, plan formal situations in advance.

Telephone calls

▶ Whenever you make a formal telephone call be as brief and as exact as possible.

▶ Be polite even if you are making a complaint.

▶ Don't try to impress your audience by using complicated words and phrases.

EXAMPLE:

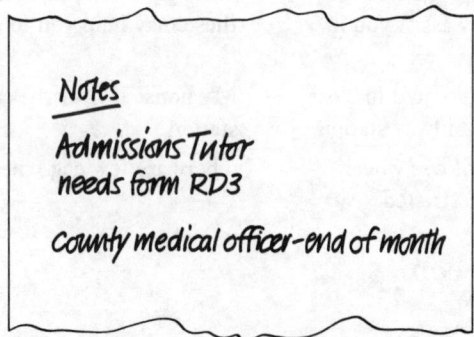

Notes

Admissions Tutor needs form RD3

county medical officer-end of month

Your telephone call might go something like this:

> "I would like to speak to the Admissions Tutor, please. I am phoning on behalf of my son Jeff Anderson. He is concerned that he hasn't received form RD3 yet as he has to send it to the County Medical Officer before the end of this month."

Interviews

Interviewer

▶ If you are interviewing someone, try to put him at his ease.

▶ Be formal, but not so formal that you intimidate your interviewee.

▶ Ask brief, clear questions.

e.g. "Could you outline what attracted you to this post?"

"How many people report directly to you in your present organisation?"

Interviewee

▸ If you are the interviewee, answer all questions as concisely, exactly and politely as possible.

▸ Give sufficient information but don't include irrelevant details.

▸ Be formal but don't try to impress your interviewer by using unnecessarily complicated vocabulary.

▸ Explain everything clearly.

e.g. If you were answering the questions above, you might say:

"I was attracted by the opportunity of running my own section. I now feel I have the necessary experience to be successful at this."

"I am directly responsible for five people in my present post: two YT trainees and three junior typists."

Meetings

▸ Always put forward your point of view clearly, politely and precisely.

▸ You want your opinions to be considered seriously, so choose effective language appropriate to the formality of the meeting.

EXAMPLE:

There are plans to build an estate of 2,500 houses on fields close to your home which is on the outskirts of a small town. A new feeder road will have to be built and it will cut across either the park or adjoining golf course. Your neighbour, Mr Hoskins, objects to these plans and puts forward his views at a local residents' meeting.

We need another new estate in Batsford like a hole in the head. It's totally crazy. There are five sites being developed in the town already. The houses in two of them are so overpriced they can't sell them and on the other three work is at a standstill because the bottom's dropped out of the economy. The council must be mad. My granddaughter and her friends play in that park, like my son before her and me before him. It's the only green space left and it's taken years to mature. It's beautiful. I don't care for that toffee-nosed lot at the golf club but live and let live I say – I don't want a road through there either.

** You agree with Mr Hoskins' objections but not with the way he expresses himself. Rewrite his speech using the same arguments but more formal language.

Votes of thanks

If you were the secretary of a small informal model-making club which meets each week in members' houses, you may offer this vote of thanks to a friend who agreed to give an informal talk to the members.

> Thanks, Alex, for giving up your time and coming to chat to us tonight. I've often heard you talk about your first attempts at racing kit cars but it was as funny tonight as the first time you told me. I could tell everyone was enjoying it from the chuckles, especially old George, I thought he was going to lay an egg.
> Cheers, mate!

As secretary of a small town horticultural society giving a vote of thanks to a radio personality, you would need to use more formal language.

> I would like to propose a vote of thanks to Ethel Tierney who so kindly agreed to join us tonight to talk about lime-loving plants.
> Your talk was most informative, interesting and entertaining. I am sure I speak on behalf of all members when I say you have provided us with a great deal to think about, and inspired us with enthusiasm and confidence. We hope we will be able to put your expert advice into practice next spring. Thank you once again for a most instructive talk.

** Look through the last vote of thanks and underline all the words and phrases which you consider contribute to the formality of the speech.

Providing information

If you give directions to someone, explain a process, give instructions or provide information on a subject:

▶ you should do so as briefly, accurately and clearly as possible;

▶ leave out any extra pieces of information or asides which may confuse the listener;

▶ give brief explanations whenever you have to use technical or unfamiliar terms.

You might give these instructions to a friend who wants to replace the timing chain on his car.

"It's a good idea to put on a new chain when you've been about 30,000 miles, or before then if you're taking the engine to bits and giving it a good going-over."

** But these instructions would be too chatty and imprecise if you were instructing a group of students. Rewrite these instructions in a more formal manner. The following words and phrases may help you.

major overhaul	renew	lower mileage
stripped down	sensible precautions	approximately

If you want to make your instructions as brief and clear as possible, you need to have a range of exact words and phrases to choose from. Listed below are some phrases which could be used for giving instructions. Some of the precise, formal vocabulary has been underlined.

Restrain the operating mechanism to avoid damage in transit

Eliminate all other causes

Align arrows A & B to open

Disperse the powder thoroughly

Ensure the plug and socket are fully engaged

Turn the screw counter clockwise

Depress buttons A & B simultaneously

Increase the flow until optimum results are obtained

Wait for the specified period

Faults may be <u>rectified</u> by <u>consulting</u> the manual

<u>Select</u> the <u>required number</u>

Take <u>suitable precautions</u>

Cover <u>located</u> at <u>rear</u>

Fill <u>appropriate</u> box

It is <u>essential</u>

** The following words can all be useful when giving instructions. Think of ways in which these words could be used.

clockwise/anti-clockwise	reduce	reserve
minimum/maximum	identify	assemble
continue/discontinue	rotate	release
connect/disconnect	control	extinguish
insert	prevent	maintain
attach	indicate	retain
replace	operate	contact
secure	aperture	circuit
interior/exterior		

In this chapter we have looked at the difference between formal and informal situations, considered when it is necessary to use formal language, and how this formality can be achieved.

13
Formal Writing

In this chapter we will consider formal writing situations and the vocabulary we can use.

Formal writing tasks

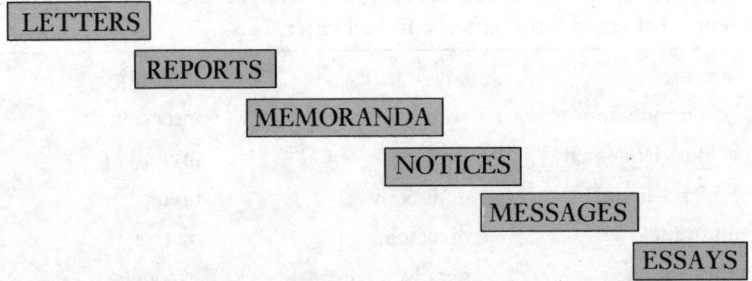

LETTERS

REPORTS

MEMORANDA

NOTICES

MESSAGES

ESSAYS

Letters

Many of us try to avoid writing formal letters by using the telephone. However, there will be occasions when it is advisable to have a permanent record, so you will need to put it in writing.

In formal letters:

▶ Be polite, sincere, exact, concise, accurate and informative
▶ Avoid colloquial words and phrases
▶ Use precise, formal vocabulary
▶ Don't try to be unnecessarily formal
▶ Avoid unnecessary words and phrases
▶ Avoid 'officialese'

Officialese is the name given to the unnecessarily complicated and contorted language which people sometimes use in business letters and official documents.

EXAMPLES:

I am in receipt of your communication dated . . .

I will reply forthwith.

Section 3

13

My company respectfully requests that . . .

I beg to acknowledge your esteemed order . . .

The best English is simple and direct; the worst is verbose and obscure. This applies to any writing situation.

To write effective formal letters you should make a plan and be prepared to write a rough draft. Whether you are writing letters as part of your private life or business letters as part of your working life, the same words and phrases keep appearing. If you are familiar with some of these, and 'know the form', it will be easier to write formal letters.

Useful words and phrases

** Look carefully at the words listed below and for each one compose a sentence that could form part of a formal letter.

accept	convenient	intention
accommodation	convenience	interview
acknowledgement	deduct	invitation
advertisement	deduction	invoice
allowances	dispatch	matter
application	details	particulars
assure	employee	personal
attached	employer	personnel
attention	employment	position
availability	effective	provided
available	enquiry (or inquiry)	punctual
benefit	enthusiastic	qualifications
catalogue	exempt	refer
circumstances	exemption	reference
complain	experience	reply
complaint	grateful	replying
conscientious	immediate	responsibility
consider	immediately	service
consideration	implications	situation
contact	inform	testimonial
contribute	information	vacancy
contribution	intend	viable

When you receive letters, note down additional words which could be useful to you when you write formal letters. Obviously, the list above is very general; the choice of words you need depends on the situation and on the purpose of your letter.

Some of the words in the list opposite have been used in the phrases given below. Many of them could be used as opening sentences for letters. If you dislike writing formal letters, it may be because you worry about how to begin your letter. By having a variety of opening sentences at your disposal, you may find it easier to write formal letters.

EXAMPLES:

I would be grateful if you could . . .

I refer to your letter of July 1st in which . . .

I wish to apply for the post/position/vacancy of . . .

I wish to complain about . . .

I read Miss Read's letter in last week's edition of the *Courier* in which she referred to . . .

Thank you for your order which we received on August 2nd . . .

I am sorry that you found cause to complain about . . .

I would be grateful if you could provide me with information about/send me details of . . .

I intend to seek further advice on this matter as . . .

While I am concerned to hear of the problem you have experienced, I . . .

We would like to offer you the opportunity of . . .

I wish to inform you . . .

I wish to be considered for . . .

I am available for interview . . .

The advertisement stated . . .

I wish to enquire about . . .

Although I have no previous experience, I . . .

As the budget is overspent, it will not be possible to carry out . . .

The work has now been satisfactorily completed and . . .

If you have any queries or would like more information . . .

Please do not hesitate to contact me (if) . . .

If you want any additional help with letter writing, there is more advice in the *Writing* book in this *Getting to Grips* series.

13

Here is an example of a formal letter.

Electronic Services

Clapton Buildings, Ranch Street, Whitton, Middlesex TW2 3JP

Ref. MK/DC

Miss R. Cole

Chatsworth Industries

Bladon

Oxon

OX43 3RP

Dear Miss Cole

Re: Monitoring Progress Results

The results of the recent Monitoring Progress
exercise for your division are listed below.
Please refer to the sheet attached which is
provided to assist you in understanding the
implications for your division.

MR2	16%
SR1	84%
ZM4	70%
PX1	49.5%
UM7	18%

If you have any queries, please contact Carole
Haydock on extension 201.

Yours sincerely

Heather Barford

Heather Barford
Divisional Secretary, Central Services

** The situation and audience demand that the following letter be formal. Rewrite the 'chatty' letter in a formal style.

UMBRELLA INSURANCE

4 MAIDERVALE ROAD
REDCAR
CLEVELAND
TS9 5SH
Tel 1642 64921

December 14th 1992

L Pemberton

2 Scott Road

Stratford Junction

Sparkhill

Birmingham

BN12 5BR

HOUSEHOLDERS' PACK
RENEWAL DATE 30.12.92
SINGLE PREMIUM DUE £178.95
or 12 PREMIUMS OF £24.90

Dear Mr Pemberton

It's now time for your insurance to be paid. As you know, it happens every year at this time. You can carry on your insurance if you pay the one-off payment which I've written down for you. I've also given you all the other prices for paying in other ways.

As there're so many claims nowadays and the cost of putting them right is going up all the time, we have got to put up our charges for small boats, caravans, horses, ponies, etc. You will see that your new cost shows this.

Yours sincerely

R Judd

Renewals Manager

Section 3

13

** Using the situation outlined below, write a formal letter of complaint to the washing machine manufacturer. Include all the information provided and use words from the vocabulary listed below.

> Your 'Benpoint de Luxe E A3131' washing machine caught fire yesterday. It's two years old. The entire load of washing scorched or burnt – can't save any of it. You were frightened by the fire. You smelt it from the garden. You're worried it could happen again. Engineer came – mended machine – and said, "It's your fault. You're not using enough powder. You don't have the machine serviced each year. Your pressure system is blocked." You said, "I'm using it properly. I follow the instructions in the handbook." In your letter, outline your claim for the cost of the burnt washing.

Vocabulary

articles	disturbing	operating instructions
items	fault	accident
inconvenient	diagnosed	satisfactorily
develop	similar	concerned
problems	recommends	fortunate
removed	insufficient	regularly
subsequent	yearly	advice
incident	manufacturer	

Reports

In most writing tasks we adopt a direct, personal approach using
▶ personal pronouns (I, you, we, etc.) and
▶ active verbs.

e.g. I suggest we adopt the flexitime system.

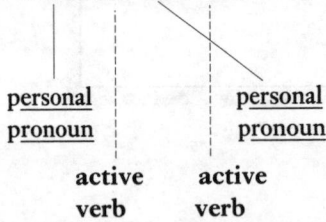

personal   personal
pronoun   pronoun

active   active
verb   verb

In report writing we use the indirect, impersonal style using

▶ impersonal pronouns (it, one, etc.) and

▶ passive verbs.

e.g. It was suggested that the flexitime system be adopted

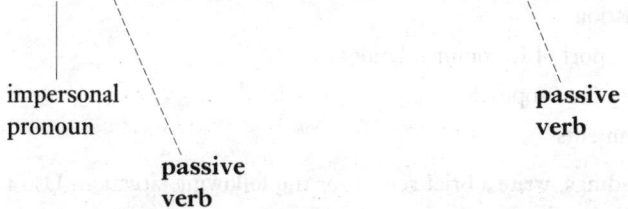

impersonal   passive
pronoun   verb

                **passive
                verb**

In reports, we adopt the indirect,

                           impersonal,

                           formal approach.

The same approach can also be used in some business letters and other official documents, depending on the situation.

** Look carefully at this extract from a job description. It was written by an employee for his departmental manager. It follows the firm's style – although the employee is writing about his own job, he writes about it in an impersonal way. Underline all the words and phrases you consider formal.

> The post holder must allocate all typing duties to other members of the Administration Section and is responsible for the quality of all typed documents, for ensuring that deadlines are met and for maintaining strict levels of confidentiality in all matters.
>
> Daily liaison with the Co-ordinator of Support Services is necessary to establish a fair division of work between the two sections: Administration and Support Services. The reception area is the direct responsibility of the post holder and customer care guidelines should be complied with at all times.
>
> All necessary staff training must be arranged and delivered by the post holder, namely, training in Health and Safety and updating computer software courses. The post holder must comply with the provisions of the Data Protection Act and ensure that all staff within the section implement the policy.

13

** Write a similar job description for your own job or your 'ideal' job. Use the same impersonal, formal approach.

Here are the main headings taken from a firm's 'house style' for reports.

Purpose of Report

Recommendation

Details in Support of Recommendations

Implementing the Proposals

Closing Comments

** Using these headings, write a brief report for the following situation. Use a formal, impersonal style.

Your company decides to look at the possibility of banning smoking at work for a trial period of six months. Its employees have put forward their views at meetings and have completed questionnaires.

The main conclusions are that each department will vote on its attitude toward the temporary ban. If the majority within a department want smoking banned, then smokers will be allowed to smoke only in special rooms: there will be one room on each floor. If a department votes not to ban smoking, smokers can continue to smoke in the office although it is hoped they will be encouraged to use the smoking rooms instead. The manager and the health and safety representative for each department will be responsible for seeing the policy is carried out. They will report to the Health Monitoring Policy Group in six months' time and the company will look at its policy again.

Memoranda

One is called a memorandum; the plural is memoranda but the abbreviations memo and memos are generally used. Memos are used at work to convey information in a brief and formal manner between one individual or department and another. They are often written on specially designed memo forms and there may be a 'house style' which employees must follow.

When writing a memo, remember to:

▶ be brief;

▶ be exact;

▶ use formal vocabulary.

MEMORANDUM

TO: All Section Heads   Date: 13.11.92.

FROM: Andy Shaw

SUBJECT: Car Parking

A new barrier will be erected at East Wing Car Park on Friday January 20th. All staff will be issued with a key which can be obtained from my secretary in room A214 between 1pm and 2pm on January 16th and 17th. A deposit of £5 must be paid for each key.

** Using the memo format provided, write a memo to a colleague who has asked for the start of his leave year to be changed. He wants it to start on September 1st in future. You agree and write a memo to him outlining your agreement. Be brief and exact.

TOWCESTER HEALTH AUTHORITY

MEMORANDUM

To: From:

Date:

Subject: _____

13

Notices

A notice should be brief and clearly laid out so that it attracts attention and can be easily read. Some notices have eye-catching graphics to suit the situation, e.g. advertising a town's firework display. Here we will consider formal notices, the type you may be required to write at work. Choice of exact, formal vocabulary will enable you to write a clear, informative and effective notice.

** Use suitable headings, numbered points and the vocabulary provided to write a fire procedure notice. Include the following information.

> If the fire's small, try and put it out yourself. If it's too large, ring the fire bell. When the bell rings, go down the stairs – the ones closest to you but you shouldn't go in the lifts. Go by the way that is marked. You must take your visitors too. Pull the doors to as you go. Go to the spot where everyone should meet – at the main gate. The most important person should see someone phones 999 and see if all the staff are at the gate.

Vocabulary

initiate	roll call	sound
extinguish	discover	descend
staircase	alarm	marked
hand-operated appliance	attempt	follow
nearest	responsible	close
senior member of staff	assembly point	direct
behind	immediately	report

Messages

We often write informal messages for members of our family and friends. So long as they are understood, it doesn't matter how we lay them out or how chatty we are in them. If we have to leave messages for colleagues at work, although the style may be less formal than in a memo, messages must be clearly laid out, brief and precise, so exact vocabulary is needed.

TO: _Phil Oscroft_

DATE: _14·11·92_   TIME: _3pm._

WHILE YOU WERE OUT

Mr _Robin Seager_

OF _Personnel_

PHONE   AREA CODE NUMBER   EXTENSION

                                _323_

TELEPHONED	✓	PLEASE CALL	
CALLED TO SEE YOU		WILL CALL AGAIN	
WANTS TO SEE YOU		URGENT	
RETURNED YOUR CALL			

MESSAGE

Wants you to include a paragraph on budget cuts in your report. Details available from M.P.T. office.

SIGNATURE _S. Timmons_

** A prospective student, A. Tarrant, phoned and asked to leave a message for R. Richards. He wants somewhere to live next term. He needs a list of places. His home address is on the form he filled in when he applied to college.

Complete the message pad overleaf. Your message should be brief and businesslike.

13

```
TO: _____
DATE: _____          TIME: _____


                    WHILE YOU WERE OUT

M _____
OF _____
PHONE      AREA CODE  NUMBER      EXTENSION

─────────────────────────────────────────────

TELEPHONED        □      PLEASE CALL         □
CALLED TO SEE YOU □      WILL CALL AGAIN     □
WANTS TO SEE YOU  □      URGENT              □
RETURNED YOUR CALL □

─────────────────────────────────────────────

                      MESSAGE

_____

_____

_____

_____

SIGNATURE
```

Essays

Unless we are at school, college, following a course of formal studies or doing examinations, we are rarely called upon to write an essay. If we return to studying, we often find essay writing difficult as the skills we once had have 'rusted' through lack of use.

In an essay you may need to:

be descriptive

be imaginative

outline a process or event

argue a point of view

An essay is often the supreme test of our formal writing skills. An essay must:

be well planned

have a logical order

fully answer the question

be relevant

contain well-chosen, precise, formal vocabulary

contain a wide variety of words and phrases

It should contain no:

colloquial words or phrases

jargon

clichés

tautology

verbosity

If you need to write an essay, follow the advice given about formal vocabulary in this chapter and go back to the advice given in previous chapters.

Chapter 8 told you about colloquial words and words more suited to informal conversation than formal writing. It suggested a variety of words that can be used to replace conversational words. Chapter 9 encouraged you to use a more varied vocabulary, shunning the familiar words whose meanings have become blunted in favour of a range of more exact and stimulating alternatives. Chapter 10 presented you with a 'paint-box' of words which, if used correctly, allows you to express your ideas and observations vividly and accurately.

The advice given in these chapters, together with sensible use of a thesaurus and the vocabulary you have gained from wide and active reading, will enable you to use a miscellany of exact and interesting words in an essay.

Final thoughts

This chapter has allowed you to put your vocabulary skills into practice in a range of formal writing situations. We hope that by working through these tasks you have gained confidence in your ability to use formal language.

With practice, your confidence should continue to grow and you should begin to feel more satisfied with your results and gain more pleasure from formal writing tasks. Whenever you are worried about formal writing, come

13

back to this chapter, look through the lists of words and phrases and see if they can help you. Be a more active reader. Take notice of the words and phrases others use in their formal writing and note down any which may be useful to incorporate into your writing at a future date. Remember, you will discover bad practice as well as good, so be discerning.

14
Over to You

Now you have worked through this book, we hope you feel that your vocabulary has increased and that you have the necessary confidence to put this new vocabulary to work. The process of acquiring new words should not end here. By now, you should be developing more active listening and reading skills and you will be accustomed to using a dictionary and thesaurus to research each unfamiliar word you encounter. This is a habit which will last you a lifetime. Above all, we trust you have developed a love of words and a curiosity which will inspire you to learn more about words, their meanings, uses and origins.

In Chapter 2 you were introduced to a range of unusual dictionaries. There are many other books which provide fascinating insights into vocabulary and language.

e.g. *A Dictionary of Misunderstood, Misused, Mispronounced Words* (ed. Laurence Urdang, published by Nelson) lists and defines words whose meanings are obscure.

A Dictionary of New English (published by Longman) lists terms, meanings and acronyms which have entered the vocabulary during the period 1963–1972.

The Scrabble Book (by Derryn Hinch, published by Pan) introduces you to a variety of unusual words with the aim of making you a better Scrabble player.

Test Your Own Wordpower (by Hunter Diack, published by Paladin) considers different aspects of vocabulary, allows you to 'test' your own vocabulary and provides you with the opportunity to encounter unfamiliar words.

Word Power (from the Readers' Digest) contains vocabulary 'tests' in which you select the correct answer from four possible alternatives. Answers are provided and you are often shown the derivation of the key word.

Word-Watching (by Philip Howard, published by Elm Tree Books) contains a wealth of unusual words.

Egg on Your Interface – A Dictionary of Modern NonSense (by Patrick Scrivenor, published Buchan & Enright) is a book about words which will make you laugh.

Boost Your Vocabulary (by J. G. Barton, published by Paperfronts) contains a series of vocabulary tests.

Making Sense of Foreign Words in English (by John Ayto, published by Chambers) explains foreign terms in general use in English.

Neo-Words – A Dictionary of the Newest and Most Unusual Words of Our Time (by David K. Barnhart, published by Collier Books).

The more you learn about the English language, the more you will want to learn. An enquiring mind will keep your love of words alive and your vocabulary will expand and flourish.

Understanding the Terms

synonym, a word which has the same or similar meaning to another word.

antonym, a word which has the opposite meaning to another word.

thesaurus, a book containing a collection of synonyms, related words and antonyms.

guide words, words which appear in bold at the top of a page in a dictionary or dictionary thesaurus which indicate the first and last complete entries on that page.

headword, (usually in bold type) a word which introduces each entry in a dictionary or dictionary thesaurus.

root word, a base word before a prefix and/or suffix is added.

prefix, a group of letters added to the beginning of a word. A prefix affects or alters the meaning of the root word.

suffix, a group of letters added to the end of a root word so making that word the correct part of speech for the sentence.

vowels, the letters a, e, i, o and u.

consonants, the remaining 21 letters of the alphabet.

singular, one item.

plural, more than one item.

syllable, a word or part of a word that can be made by one effort of breath.

stress, the part of a word which is emphasised.

noun, naming word used to identify a person, place, animal or thing.

adjective, a word which describes or gives more information about a noun.

verb, a word which expresses an action or a state of being.

adverb, a word which gives more information about a verb.

pronoun, a word used instead of a noun.

preposition, usually introduces a phrase containing a noun or pronoun and shows the relationship between this noun or pronoun and another word in the sentence.

I.P.A. (International Phonetic Alphabet), symbols used as a pronunciation guide.

reading skills:

    <u>skimming</u>, allows the reader to gain a general impression of the text.

    <u>scanning</u>, allows the reader to search for a particular item in a text.

    <u>context cueing</u>, allows the reader to guess words from the setting they appear in.

colloquial language, words used in informal speech.

cliché, a stereotyped expression.

tautology, an unnecessary repetition of the same idea in different words.

verbosity, wordiness.

draft, a preliminary outline for a piece of writing.

Answers

NB No answers are given where you are asked to research words in a dictionary or thesaurus, where answers depend upon personal responses, or where a number of alternative answers is possible.

Chapter 2   Understanding Dictionaries

Understanding abbreviations and symbols

bizarre – stress the second syllable

harry – stress the first syllable

nibble – stress the first syllable

primitive – stress the first syllable

municipal – stress the second syllable

pompom – stress the first syllable

Parts of speech

cavernous – adjective

collude – verb

furtively – adverb

caucus – noun

ruminate – verb

Chapter 3   Using Dictionaries

Different meanings

taint (verb)

  – to infect

  – to go bad

  – to contaminate

manacle (noun)

  – a handcuff

  – a restraint for the hands

exodus (noun)

  – departure of many people

eddy (noun)

  – a small whirlpool or whirlwind

mellow (adjective)

  – soft and ripe

  – soft to touch, taste or hear

  – well-matured

exhume (verb)

  – to unearth or dig out

donor (noun)
- person who provides blood, tissue, an organ or semen
- a giver

nonchalant (adjective)
- unconcerned, unmoved,
- unexcited, indifferent

gregarious (adjective)
- fond of company
- living in flocks, herds, communities

deign (verb)
- condescend
- think fit to

Final thoughts
Suggested answers
malignant – harmful
oblique – slanting
flurries – gusts, blasts, squalls
assaulted – attacked, stormed
obliterating – blotting out, effacing, destroying, erasing
frenetic – frantic, delirious
atoms – particles
fractured – splintered

Chapter 4 Using a Thesaurus

Roget's Thesaurus
Suggested synonyms

1 The child was admonished/chastised/chided/rebuked/reproached/reproved/scolded by his parents.

2 It is anticipated/envisaged/predicted that inflation will start to drop/decline/decrease by the autumn.

3 The gleaming/glossy/glistening green leaves provided a good contrast to the brilliant/dazzling/vivid/colourful flowers.

4 Her writing was very tidy/meticulous.

5 The match was long and dull/monotonous/tedious/unexciting/uninteresting/wearisome; most of the spectators had left before the final whistle.

6 I regret to advise/notify/tell you that you were unsuccessful on this occasion.

Suggested antonyms

lucky – unfortunate, unlucky, untimely

heroic – cowardly, craven, base, ignoble

clever – dull, slow, stupid, unintelligent

begin – cease, finish, complete, end, stop, terminate

bitter – sweet, sugary, pleasant

grow – decline, decrease, diminish

reluctant – eager, enthusiastic, keen, willing

hesitant – resolute, determined

To improve your writing and speaking skills
Suggested choices

want – wish

protest – complain

got – bought

components – ingredients

says – states

has – contains

think – imagine or believe

normally – usually

return – refund

Chapter 6 Reading and Understanding

Context

1 calumny – slanderous statement, malicious gossip

2 capricious – liable to sudden changes of mind, not governed by judgement

3 emulate – imitate, rival, try to equal

4 heinous – atrocious

5 hiatus – break, pause

Related words

1 Both words are to do with lacking something.

2 These words relate to equality.

3 All three words are to do with producing an effect, usually in a beneficial sense.

4 These words mean having impulse.

5 These four words are to do with feelings.

6 Two words whose meanings revolve around knowing.

Cloze procedure

Suggested answers

Without doubt the long hot summer of 1990 took its toll in terms of increases in the number of reported thefts and burglaries.

Figures for the second quarter of 1990 showed a 17% rise in recorded crime with marked increases in burglary and car crime.

These figures/statistics paint a gloomy picture, but what is even more depressing is that many of these crimes are opportunistic and would not have happened if people had been more aware. For example, a third of domestic burglaries did not involve forced entry as the householder had left a door or window open.

Basic crime prevention costs little; in most/many cases it costs nothing except your time. There are various measures you can take to stop yourself being the victim of the opportunist.

Multiple choice comprehension

1 d early autumn or late spring

2 a moist soil and atmosphere and sheltered position

3 a are found as far as the east side of the Rockies

4 c long straight-grain timbers of substantial cross-section.

Chapter 7 Get It Right

Colloquial language

He's always causing trouble.

It's inconvenient

The company has introduced some ill-considered ideas recently.

It seems risky to me.

She has a weak heart.

Did you see her?

Clichés

The clichés in the article have been underlined.

> ## COUNCIL ANNOUNCES SPENDING BREAKTHROUGH
>
> Yesterday Councillor E Smith announced cuts in spending amounting to a staggering £200,000. "These savings have been made," Councillor Smith declared, "by swingeing cuts in costs. No stone has been left unturned. Every avenue explored. In this day and age, our residents have a right to expect the Council to come up with a blueprint for success to ensure high standards of service at a rock bottom price."

Tautology

The unnecessary word has been underlined in the sentences below.

1 The two teams combined together to raise money for charity.

2 He repeated the word again.

3 It was necessary to separate the two dogs apart.

4 The doctor mentioned about the surgery's closure next week.

5 The electricity supply has been connected up.

Chapter 8   Conversational Words

mad

Your synonyms for 'anger' may include the following.

rage	displeasure	vexation
exasperation	irritation	annoyance
fury	outrage	indignation

tell off

Suggestions

1 The new recruit was <u>disciplined</u> by the colour sergeant.

2 As Lisa had forgotten to post his letter, he would <u>scold</u> her in the morning.

3 The timid student was embarrassed by the <u>admonishment</u> he received.

4 Nigel was accustomed to being <u>lectured</u> for minor misdemeanours.

5 He hated being <u>reprimanded</u> in front of his friends.

6 Alex was frequently accused of <u>nagging</u> his wife.

fed up

1 The elderly tourist was <u>nauseated by</u> the sight of so many undernourished children.

2 Ursula was <u>annoyed by</u>/<u>vexed by</u> his interference and his unwelcome offers of help.

3 The receptionist was <u>vexed by</u>/<u>annoyed by</u> her supervisor's attitude.

4 The nurse was <u>worn out by</u> climbing the four flights of stairs to the pharmacy.

Replacing 'boring'

dull and commonplace	humdrum
causing annoyance	irksome
never changing	unvaried
happening over and over again	repetitious
not holding the attention	uninteresting
no longer fresh	stale

Replacing 'funny', meaning 'amusing'

synonyms	antonyms
mirth-provoking	humourless
droll	serious
hilarious	sad
ludicrous	
ridiculous	
absurd	

great

exquisite	of outstanding delicacy or beauty
exemplary	worthy of notice or imitation
meritorious	deserving honour or reward
eminent	distinguished, rising above all others
superlative	superior to all others

Antonyms for 'excellent'

substandard

imperfect

faulty

inferior

damaged

lots of

1 10,000

2 too many to count

3 abundant

kind of and sort of

Suggested answers

1 In a way, Mike expected Clara to refuse.

2 I dislike his quasi-aggressive manner.

3 My friends have seemingly ignored me since I went to work in Exeter.

4 Mrs Owen imposed a certain discipline on her two sons.

5 Lizzy was rather confused when Graham invited her to stay for the weekend.

hard and difficult

simple	uncomplicated
effortless	straightforward
undemanding	clear
achievable	attainable

dear

cheap

reasonable

bargain

affordable

economical

give up

Suggested answers

1 He had to <u>abandon/relinquish</u> all thoughts of a career in the police... .

2 The small band of rebels was forced to <u>surrender/capitulate</u>.

3 It was time to <u>resign</u> his commission in the army.

4 Rachel decided to <u>cede</u> her place in the team to a younger player.

5 If you do not <u>desist/cease</u> interfering, you will be sacked.

6 Placing his hand on the Bible, he swore that he would <u>forswear</u> his criminal practices.

Chapter 9   'Faded' Words

nice

Suggestions

1 a polite/refined/courteous child

2 a precise/exact/careful essay

3 a pretty/attractive/handsome/pleasant face

4 a becoming/suitable/well-cut/flattering dress

gorgeous	exquisite
captivating	engaging
gratifying	alluring
appealing	winning
radiant	ravishing

nasty

Adding prefixes

unattractive   disagreeable

displeasing   unenjoyable

          unappealing

Suggested definitions

lewd – lustful

noisome – likely to injure health, disgusting to see or smell

repellent – distasteful

loathsome – arousing hate or disgust

obnoxious – objectionable

vicious – spiteful, ill-tempered

malicious – driven by hatred or spite

malodorous – ill-smelling

odious – hateful, repulsive

repugnant – distasteful, disgusting

despicable – holding in contempt

unsavoury – offensive

surly – gruff and grumpy

Suggested answers

1 foul/disgusting weather

2 repellent/malodorous/noisome smell

3 unappetizing/revolting taste

4 vicious/surly temper

5 obscene/offensive/indecent language

6 polluted/noisome pool of stagnant water

good

Suggestions

1 bright/cloudless/balmy/calm weather

2 appetizing/satisfying/wholesome food

3 clever/capable/thorough student

4 precious/valuable bracelet

5 commendable/praiseworthy decision

6 abundant/plentiful/sizeable crop of strawberries

bad

1 Even Lee's friends described him as a naughty/wayward/disobedient boy because he was always being punished for his misdeeds.

2 On their return, they discovered that the food in the faulty refrigerator was rancid/putrid/mouldy.

3 Their grave/disastrous financial position had been caused by the recession.

4 I feel guilty/upset/contrite about your house being broken into when I was supposed to be looking after it.

5 Phil Thomas has chronic asthma and was unable to attend the committee meeting because he was ill/unwell.

strange

1 My cousin is looking forward to visiting a foreign country.

2 Braithwaite rarely scored many runs on an unfamiliar pitch.

3 She felt bewildered and uncertain of what to do.

4 I am unaccustomed to this department.

5 The boy scout felt disorientated – he had lost his sense of direction.

6 The plan was to visit unexplored parts of the jungle.

7 His remarkable powers impressed his audience.

big or large and little or small

1 a plentiful/abundant yield
2 a spacious/roomy/sizeable house
3 a bulky parcel
4 a burly man
5 a powerful/influential statesman
6 a considerable/substantial inheritance

little or small

trivial	unimportant
negligible	insignificant
inadequate	insufficient

old and young

1 infant
2 adolescent
3 immature
4 juvenile
5 junior
6 fledgling
7 childish
8 infantile
9 puerile

interesting

Suggestions

1 a stimulating television programme
2 an intriguing book
3 an engrossing/riveting/absorbing film
4 a fascinating/compelling play
5 a captivating/spell-binding pantomime
6 a provocative comment

rich and poor

1 opulent, sumptuous

2 lavish

3 affluent, wealthy, prosperous

4 fertile, productive, fruitful

5 plentiful, abundant

6 lush, luxuriant

7 creamy, flavoursome, tasty, delicious, juicy, succulent

8 deep, warm, strong, vivid, bright

9 full, mellow, resonant, deep

Suggestions

1 poor (with little money) – needy, impoverished, poverty-stricken, destitute, penniless, impecunious

2 poor soil – infertile, unproductive

3 poor supply of food – scanty, inadequate, deficient, paltry, insufficient

4 poor quality – inferior, substandard, faulty, unsatisfactory

like and don't like

Suggested nouns

loathing, aversion, execration, repulsion, detestation, antipathy, enmity, antagonism, animosity, abomination, abhorrence

got and get

Avoiding 'get' and 'got':

Suggestions

1 Shirley gained/obtained top marks in her swimming examination.

2 My neighbour won/was awarded first prize for her roses.

3 I have solved/discovered the answer to the problem.

4 My sister possesses/owns a yacht and a dinghy.

5 Sybil's brother contracted/caught malaria when he was in Africa.

6 Will you fetch/collect the children from school for me?

7 He was involved in a fight on Saturday.

8 The teenager <u>climbed on</u>/<u>leapt on</u> his bike and <u>escaped</u>.

9 I will go to the library to <u>find</u>/<u>borrow</u> a book about Dryden.

10 Joan's mother can usually <u>persuade</u>/<u>coax</u> her to mow the lawn.

11 As you <u>approach</u>/<u>near</u> the church, it is on your right.

12 The coach will <u>arrive at</u>/<u>reach</u> Manchester at 15.30.

13 If you work hard, you will <u>succeed</u>/<u>prosper</u>.

14 My father <u>inherited</u> a considerable amount of money when his aunt died.

15 If you can <u>survive</u>/<u>overcome</u>/<u>endure</u> the initial feeling of nausea, you will enjoy the experience.

Colloquial phrases:

Suggestions

1 I can <u>manage</u> with just a few words of Italian.

2 February always <u>depresses me</u>.

3 My son has always been able to <u>join in</u>/<u>participate in</u> any party or outing.

4 If only I could <u>explain</u>/<u>successfully communicate</u> my feelings to my father.

5 My grandmother has plenty of <u>energy</u>/<u>vitality</u> for her age.

6 Maria felt he was always <u>mocking</u>/<u>criticising</u>/<u>making fun of</u> her.

Chapter 10   Shades of Meaning

quiet

Suggestions

1 a calm/motionless sea

2 an unpretentious/simple wedding

3 a subdued/meek/shy child

4 a hushed/isolated wood

antonyms for 'quiet'

1 a restless/turbulent sea

2 a high-spirited/impatient/passionate personality

3 conspicuous/ostentatious/showy clothing

4 a restless/turbulent/violent city

happy

Suggestions

Sarah was content/overjoyed/elated when her baby was born.

Mike walked along the road, pleased/delighted/glad to be out in the fresh air once more after his long day at work.

I was gratified/delighted to be awarded first prize.

The joyous/jubilant civilians waved to the soldiers who had liberated their town.

The children's merry/cheerful laughter showed their enjoyment of the puppet show.

Antonyms for 'happy'

forlorn	sombre	melancholy
despondent	miserable	mournful

cold

Suggestions

On a winter's day . . .

the weather was bleak, biting, raw, frosty, glacial, wintry

the people were indifferent, aloof, phlegmatic, unresponsive, frigid, undemonstrative

I was numbed, chilly, chilled, shivery, frozen to the bone/marrow, icy, frozen

A passionate person is . . .

fiery	animated
emotional	vital
impetuous	impulsive

empty

Suggestions

1 Rodney reviewed his <u>aimless</u>/<u>idle</u>/<u>futile</u> life and regretted the wasted opportunities.

2 The children, having removed all the decorations, surveyed the <u>bare</u> room.

3 The <u>uninhabited</u> countryside looked bleak in the cold winter light.

4 A <u>futile</u>/<u>trivial</u>/<u>banal</u> gesture is not worth making.

5 She sat looking at the <u>blank</u> paper, willing herself to write.

Alternatives to 'empty'

consume	vacate	evacuate
drain	deplete	exhaust

full

Suggestions

1 The towel was <u>saturated with</u> water.

2 His <u>detailed</u>/<u>extensive</u> knowledge of Africa proved useful when they visited Zambia.

3 Her <u>ample</u>/<u>generous</u>/<u>voluptuous</u> figure caused problems when she tried to buy the latest fashions.

4 The <u>abundant</u>/<u>plentiful</u> crop of plums broke the tree's branches.

5 The student's <u>copious</u>/<u>detailed</u>/<u>extensive</u>/<u>exhaustive</u> notes helped him when it was time to revise.

heavy

onerous responsibility

solemn occasion

profuse bleeding

oppressive heat

inert body

ponderous footsteps

Antonyms for 'heavy'

slight	trivial	sparse
agile	calm	bearable

bright

Suggestions

John has a <u>dazzling</u>/<u>promising</u>/<u>brilliant</u> future before him.

It is a <u>fair</u>/<u>sunny</u>/<u>cloudless</u>/<u>glorious</u> day.

Milli is a <u>cheerful</u>/<u>vivacious</u>/<u>lively</u>/<u>intelligent</u> child.

Turn the light off. It's too <u>radiant</u>/<u>dazzling</u>/<u>intense</u>/<u>brilliant</u>.

Alternatives to 'bright'

luminous	smart	outstanding
gleaming	sparkling	glowing

dull

Suggestions

1 The <u>dismal</u>/<u>gloomy</u> weather over the holiday period caused many people to stay at home.

2 He awoke feeling <u>dismal</u>/<u>depressed</u> and lethargic.

3 Without the customary glowing fire, the room looked <u>cheerless</u> and uninviting.

4 Winston had hoped to enjoy the party but the <u>prosaic</u>/<u>stupid</u> conversation made him leave early.

5 Listening to the others' achievements, she felt <u>stupid</u>/<u>untalented</u>/<u>drab</u> and inadequate.

fat and thin

Suggestions

a rounded/chubby/bouncing baby

a gross/portly/stout/paunchy businessman

Alternatives to 'thin'

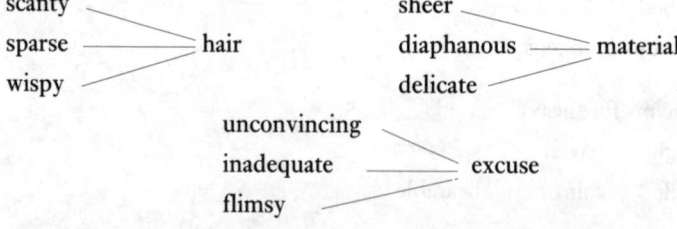

careful

chary

punctilious

heedful

scrupulous

judicious

solicitous

Suggestions

1 a cautious/vigilant driver

2 a person careful about money is concerned, particular, thrifty, prudent, scrupulous

3 a person careful in appearance is neat, discreet, fastidious, particular

4 a person careful in speech is accurate, precise, discreet, fastidious, prudent, particular, judicious

5 a person careful about others is conscientious, attentive, vigilant, concerned, solicitous

careless

1 perfunctory

2 nonchalant

3 indiscreet

Anagrams

cursory

unguarded

neglectful

artless

heedless

unmindful

offhand

unstudied

incautious

Alternatives to 'careless'

Suggestions

1 Service at that restaurant is always offhand/slapdash/casual/ perfunctory.

2 His inconsiderate/indiscreet/thoughtless/question caused her great distress.

3 The slapdash/hasty/negligent repair to the car only held for a few miles.

4 The driver gave a perfunctory/casual/nonchalant/cursory glance in his mirror before driving away.

5 James was casual/unconcerned/neglectful/heedless of his appearance.

Chapter 12   Being Formal

Making the wrong choice

The informal words and phrases are underlined; the unnecessary information is in bold.

```
                              CRAVEN SUPPLIES
                              Unit 17a
                              Piddinghoe Industrial Estate
                              East Sussex
                              BN4 3EB
                              Tel: 0962 492904


                              December 17th 1992
             Mrs E Flaherty
             Bilston Chemicals
             Reeve Lane
             Chichester
             West Sussex
             PO4 197


             Order Reference Number BM7R/294/172X

             Dear Mrs Flaherty

             Thanks for your letter. We got it yesterday. Our
             new girl's dealing with it and you'll get it
             soon. You know us — good service, prompt
             delivery.

             Don't forget, as usual, any problems or anything
             I can do for you — just give us a bell.

             As ever

             P. Lomas
             Pauline Lomas
             Divisional Manager
```

Your formal letter might read like this:

Dear Mrs Flaherty

Thank you for your letter which we received yesterday. Your order is being dealt with and you will receive it as soon as possible.

If you have any queries, please do not hesitate to telephone me.

Yours sincerely

Meetings

Your rewrite of Mr Hoskins' speech might sound like this:

> We do not need another new housing estate in Batsford as there are five existing developments. Houses on two of these sites are so expensive that buyers can't be found and work has stopped on the other sites because of lack of confidence in the economy. The proposed site, the park, is now the only green space in the town for children to play on. It would be foolhardy to destroy such beautiful, mature parkland or the public golf course by building a road through either of them.

Votes of thanks

The formal words and phrases are underlined.

I would like to propose a vote of thanks to Ethel Tierney who so kindly agreed to join us tonight to talk about lime-loving plants. Your talk was most informative, interesting and entertaining. I am sure I speak on behalf of all members when I say you have provided us with a great deal to think about, and inspired us with enthusiasm and confidence. We hope we will be able to put your expert advice into practice next spring. Thank you once again for a most instructive talk.

Providing information

Your instructions might sound like this.

"It is a sensible precaution to renew the chain at approximately 30,000 miles or at a lower mileage if the engine is stripped down for a major overhaul."

Chapter 13 Formal Writing

Letters

Your formal letter might read like this once you have rewritten it.

UMBRELLA INSURANCE

4 MAIDERVALE ROAD
REDCAR
CLEVELAND
TS9 5SH
Tel 1642 64921

December 14th 1992

> HOUSEHOLDERS' PACK
> RENEWAL DATE 30.12.92
> SINGLE PREMIUM DUE £178.95
> or 12 PREMIUMS OF £24.90

Dear Mr Pemberton

I see from our records that your policy is now due for renewal. To maintain adequate insurance cover, there are two ways to pay: by sending us a single payment of the premium due by the renewal date shown above, or in monthly payments, details of which are enclosed.

Due to an increase in the number and cost of claims, it has unfortunately become necessary for us to increase our rates for small boats, caravans, horses, ponies, etc. Your new premium, shown above, reflects these increases. Nevertheless, I do hope you will continue to find our rates competitive and to renew your cover with us.

Yours sincerely

Suggested letter to washing machine manufacturer:

Dear Sir

I wish to make a claim for several items of clothing which were damaged in my Benpoint de Luxe E A3131 washing machine yesterday. A list of the items is attached.

My washing machine worked satisfactorily until yesterday morning when, while I was working in the garden, I suddenly smelt burning. Having turned off the power and opened the washing machine door, I removed the articles and discovered that all of them were either burnt or badly scorched.

This very distressing incident was completely unexpected, as I would not have thought such a fault would develop in a machine which is only two years old. Your engineer, Alan Ball, came and diagnosed the fault as being a blocked pressure system, and fitted a replacement part. When I asked him the cause of the fault, he said I had used insufficient powder and failed to have the machine serviced each year. However, I cannot accept these as adequate reasons; I have always followed the operating instructions in the manufacturer's handbook.

I am worried that a similar incident could occur in the future and that the damage caused to the machine on this occasion may lead to related problems entailing extra repair costs.

Furthermore, it is highly inconvenient to have lost the items of clothing which were damaged in the fire and I trust you will deal with my claim promptly and reimburse me in full to the value stated on the attached list.

I look forward to hearing your comments.

Yours faithfully

Reports

The formal words and phrases are underlined.

> The post holder must allocate all typing duties to other members of the Administration Section and is responsible for the quality of all typed documents, for ensuring that deadlines are met and for maintaining strict levels of confidentiality in all matters.
>
> Daily liaison with the Co-ordinator of Support Services is necessary to establish a fair division of work between the two sections: Administration and Support Services. The reception area is the direct responsibility of the post holder and customer care guidelines should be complied with at all times.
>
> All necessary staff training must be arranged and delivered by the post holder, namely, training in Health and Safety and updating computer software courses. The post holder must comply with the provisions of the Data Protection Act and ensure that all staff within the section implement the policy.

Your report on the meeting about banning smoking could read like this:

Report on the Smoking Policy of this company, meeting held May 23rd 1992.

Purpose of Report

To consider proposals for the banning of smoking in the workplace.

Recommendations

It is recommended that there should be a six-month trial ban on smoking in all departments after employees have had the opportunity of voting on the issue.

Details in Support of Recommendations

1 If the majority of employees in a department vote to ban smoking for the trial period, smokers will be required to smoke in the rooms provided: one to be situated on each floor.

2 If the majority of employees in a department vote against a trial ban, smokers will be allowed to continue smoking in the office although they will be encouraged to use the rooms provided.

Implementing the Proposals

Departmental managers and safety representatives will be responsible for the implementation of the new policy and will be required to report their findings to the Health Monitoring Policy Group within six months.

Closing Comments

The company's policy towards banning smoking in the workplace will be reviewed in six months' time.

Memoranda

Suggestion

TOWCESTER HEALTH AUTHORITY

Memorandum

From: Sam McKnight   To: Adam Brown

Date: 27th July 1992

Subject: Change of Leave Year

I confirm that I have agreed to you changing your leave year to commence (start/begin) from September 1st.

Notices

ON DISCOVERING A FIRE

1 If the fire is small, attempt to extinguish it with a hand-operated appliance.

2 If the fire is not extinguished immediately, sound the alarm.

ON HEARING THE ALARM

1 Do not use the lift; use the nearest staircase.

2 Follow the marked escape route.

3 Close all doors behind you.

4 Staff are responsible for their visitors' safety.

5 Report to the assembly point at the main gate.

6 The most senior member of staff should:

     direct a member of staff to call the fire service (999) and

     initiate a roll call.

Messages

TO: R Richards

DATE: 27/9/92   TIME: 3.30

WHILE YOU WERE OUT

Mr A Tarrant

OF

PHONE   AREA CODE   NUMBER   EXTENSION

TELEPHONED	✓	PLEASE CALL
CALLED TO SEE YOU		WILL CALL AGAIN
WANTS TO SEE YOU		URGENT
RETURNED YOUR CALL		

MESSAGE

Mr Tarrant would like you to send him a list of addresses for recommendation for the coming term. His address is on his college application form

SIGNATURE M. Burdock

Index